Halloween Face Painting Party for Kids

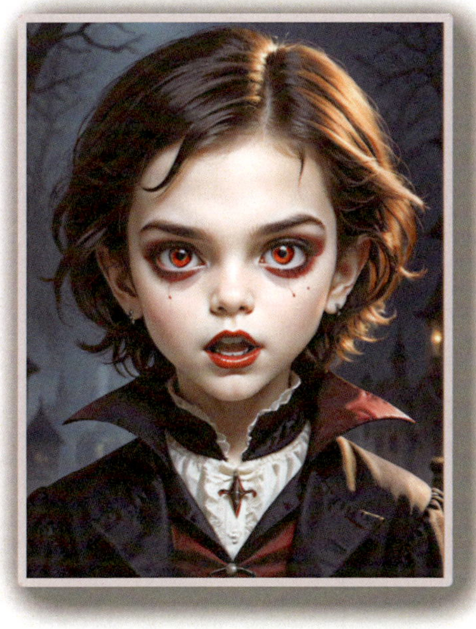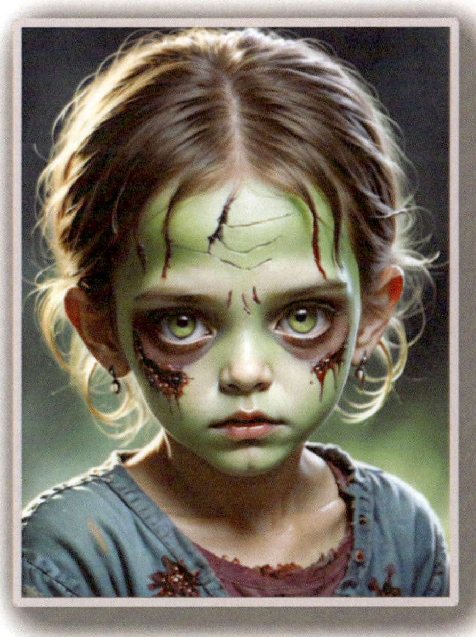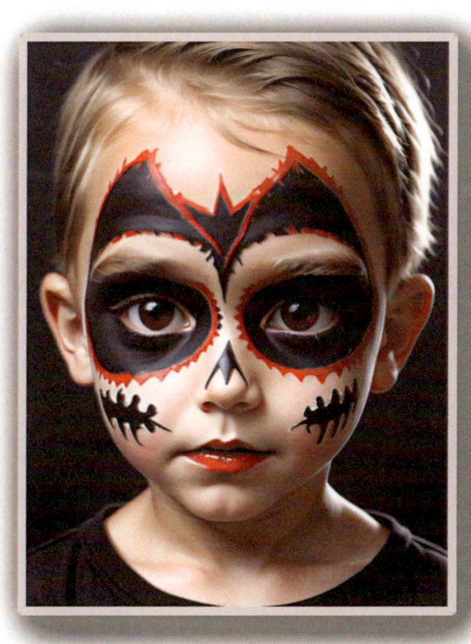

Introduction

Halloween is a time of magic, mystery, and of course, terrifying costumes! Every year, kids and adults eagerly await the chance to transform into their favorite characters — from classic zombies and devils to other dark and spooky figures. Face painting is a fantastic way to add realism and uniqueness to any costume, and it's also great fun for the whole family.

In this book, you'll find inspiration and instructions to help you create unforgettable Halloween face paintings. Whether you're a beginner face painting enthusiast or an experienced artist, our step-by-step guides will lead you through each stage of creating spooky, fun, and unique designs.

From classic designs like clowns, witches, and devils, to more intricate projects like the terrifying zombie — there's something here for everyone. No matter which theme you choose, remember that the most important thing is to have fun and be creative!

Dive into the world of Halloween and let your imagination run wild. It's time to grab your brushes, paints, and create unforgettable, creepy (or cute!) works of art on the faces of your loved ones. Make this Halloween full of colors, emotions, and magical transformations!

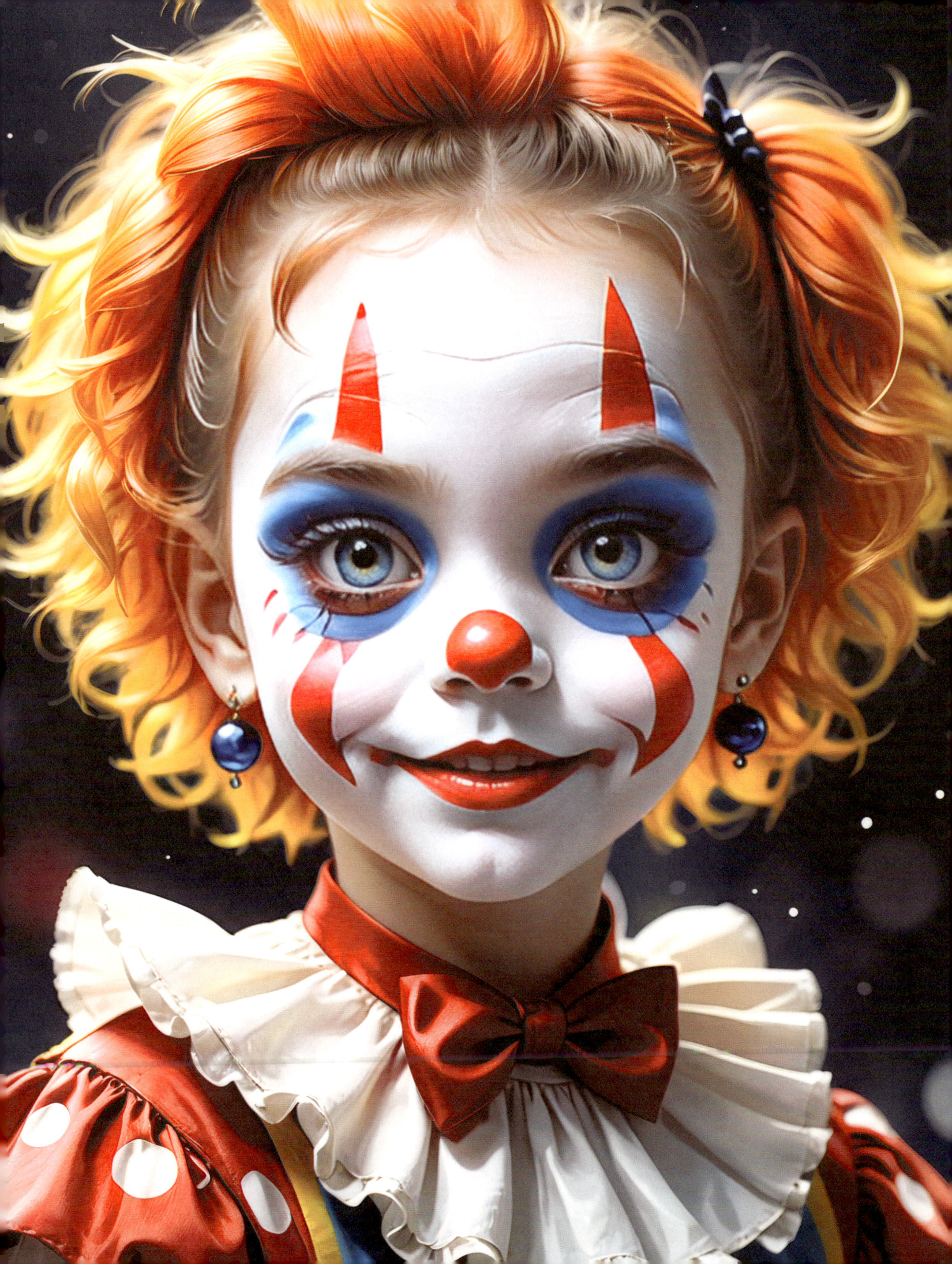

Dreamy Clown

Materials:

- Face paints: white, red, blue

- Sponge, thin and medium brushes

- Optional: bright wig, clown costume with ruffles and polka dots

Steps:

1.White Base:

Apply a smooth layer of white face paint over the entire face using a sponge as a foundation.

2.Red Clown Nose and Cheeks:

Paint a bright red circle on the nose. Apply red paint to the cheeks just above the smile lines.

3.Blue Eye Makeup:

Apply blue face paint around the eyes, extending slightly outward and upward. Blend softly and leave space between the blue paint and eyebrows.

4.Red and White Accents:

Paint two red triangles above the eyebrows and smaller ones under the eyes. Highlight with white for a 3D effect.

5.Lips:

Paint the lips with red, extending slightly beyond the corners for an exaggerated smile. Add white highlights for emphasis.

6.Final Touches:

Ensure all lines are clean. Add small stars or dots around the eyes if desired.

7.Accessories:

Pair with a bright wig and traditional clown costume to complete the look.

8.Tips:

Focus on symmetry, especially with the red triangles and blue eye makeup. Keep colors vibrant for a playful appearance.

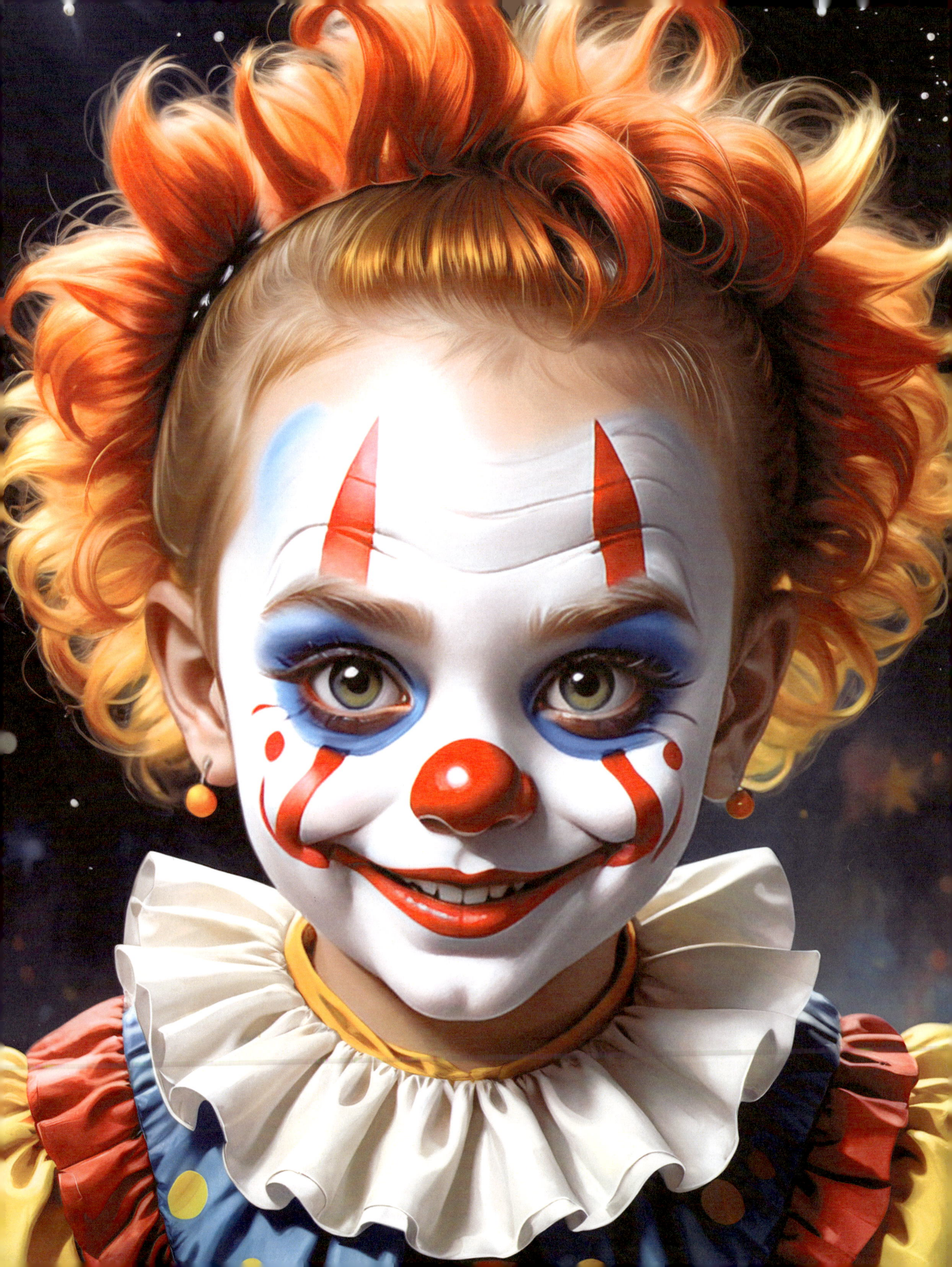

Cheerful Carnival Clown

Materials:

- Face paints: white, red, blue

- Sponge, thin and medium brushes

- Optional: bright wig, clown costume with ruffles and polka dots

Steps:

1.White Base:

Apply a smooth layer of white face paint over the entire face using a sponge as the foundation.

2.Red Clown Nose and Cheeks:

Paint a red circle on the nose. Apply red paint to the cheeks just above the smile lines for a rosy look.

3.Blue Eye Makeup:

Use a medium brush to apply blue face paint around the eyes, blending outward. Leave space between the blue paint and eyebrows.

4.Red and White Accents:

Paint two red triangles above the eyebrows and smaller ones under the eyes. Highlight with white for a 3D effect.

5.Lips:

Paint the lips with red, extending slightly beyond the corners for an exaggerated smile. Add white highlights.

6.Final Touches:

Ensure all lines are clean. Add small stars or dots around the eyes if desired.

7.Accessories:

Pair with a bright wig and traditional clown costume to complete the look.

8.Tips:

Symmetry is important, especially with the red triangles and blue eye makeup. Keep colors vibrant for a playful appearance.

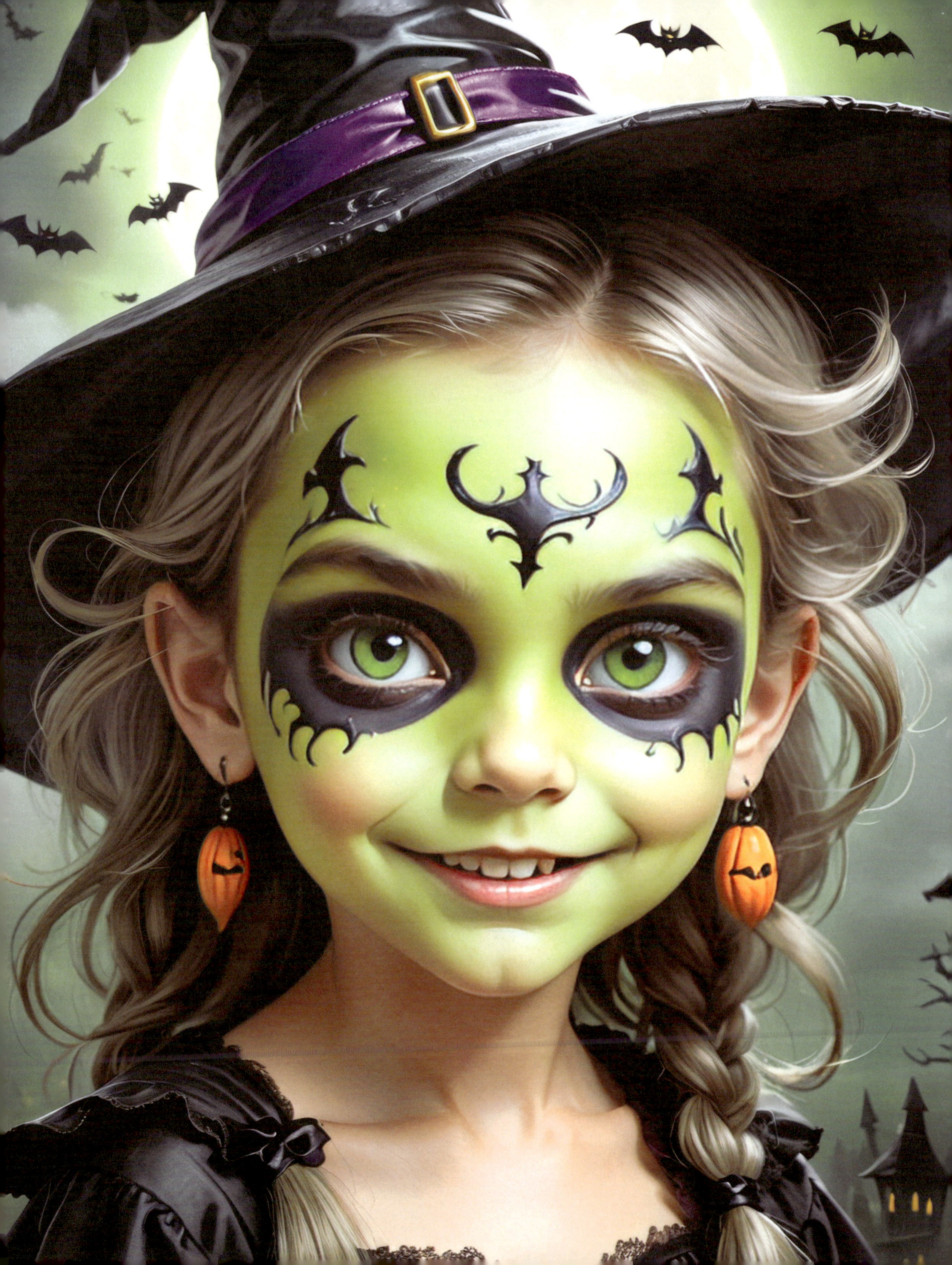

WICKED WITCH

Materials:

- Face paints: green, black

- Sponge, thin and medium brushes

- Optional: witch hat, Halloween-themed accessories (e.g., pumpkin earrings)

Steps:

1.Green Base:

Apply a smooth, even layer of green face paint over the entire face using a sponge. This creates the foundation for the witchy look.

2.Dark Eye Makeup:

Use a medium brush to apply black face paint around the eyes, creating a shadowed, dramatic look. Extend the black paint slightly outward and blend to soften the edges.

3.Forehead and Cheek Designs:

With a thin brush, paint intricate black designs on the forehead and cheeks. These could be gothic or bat-like shapes, adding to the spooky theme. Ensure symmetry between the designs on both sides of the face.

4.Lip Detail:

Apply black paint or dark lipstick to the lips, keeping the look bold and striking.

5.Final Touches:

Ensure all lines and details are sharp and well-defined, especially around the eyes and forehead.

Add any additional elements like small stars, dots, or other decorative details around the eyes if desired.

6.Accessories:

Pair the face paint with a classic witch hat and Halloween-themed accessories like pumpkin earrings to complete the look.

A black dress or witch costume will enhance the overall effect, making the look more cohesive.

7.Tips:

Focus on symmetry, particularly with the forehead and cheek designs, to maintain a balanced and polished appearance.

Keep the colors vibrant and the black details crisp to create a dramatic and enchanting witch look.

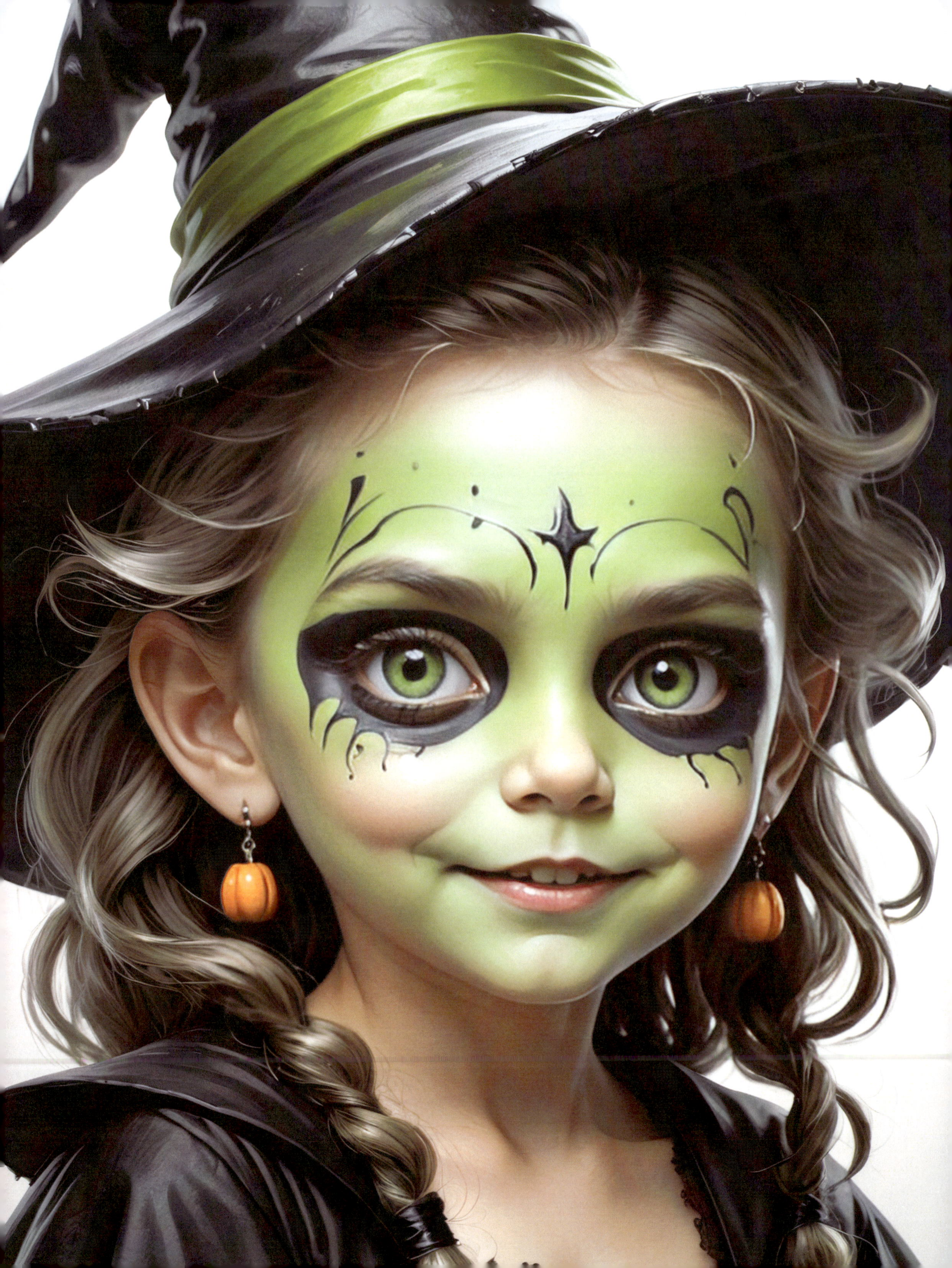

Playful Witch

Materials:

- Face paints: green, black

- Sponge, thin and medium brushes

- Optional: witch hat, Halloween-themed earrings (like pumpkins)

Steps:

1.Green Base:

Apply a smooth, even layer of green face paint over the entire face using a sponge. This will be the foundation of the witchy appearance.

2.Dark Eye Makeup:

Use a medium brush to apply black face paint around the eyes, creating a shadowed, dramatic look. Extend the black paint slightly outward and blend to soften the edges, giving the eyes a hollow, enchanting effect.

3.Forehead and Cheek Designs:

With a thin brush, paint small, delicate black designs on the forehead and under the eyes. These could resemble vines, thorns, or abstract patterns, adding to the magical and mysterious aura. Ensure the designs are symmetrical.

4.Lip Detail:

Apply a subtle touch of black or dark green lipstick to the lips, maintaining a slightly understated but mysterious look.

5.Final Touches:

Ensure all lines are sharp and well-blended, especially around the eyes and forehead. Add tiny dots or stars around the designs for extra magical flair if desired.

6.Accessories:

Pair the face paint with a classic black witch hat, and consider wearing Halloween-themed earrings, such as small pumpkins, to enhance the look.

A black dress or witch costume with subtle details will complete the ensemble, making the character appear more cohesive and enchanting.

7.Tips:

Symmetry is crucial for the designs on the forehead and around the eyes to create a balanced look.

Keep the colors vibrant and the black details crisp to achieve a polished and magical appearance.

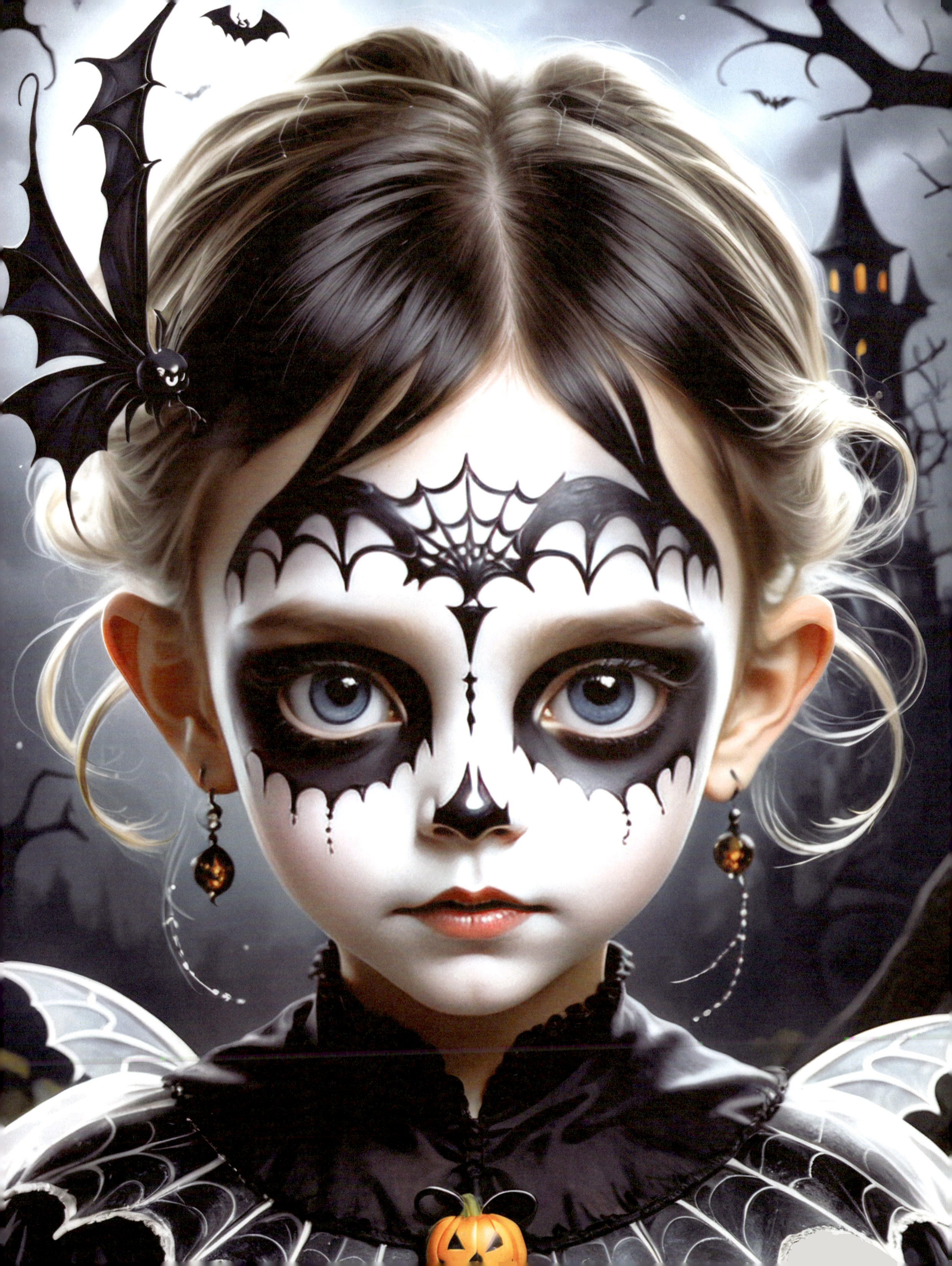

Gothic Spider Witch

Materials:

- Face paints: white, black

- Sponge, thin and medium brushes

- Optional: bat hair accessory, spider-themed costume

Steps:

1.White Base:

Apply a smooth, even layer of white face paint over the entire face using a sponge. This serves as the pale, eerie foundation for the look.

2.Black Eye Makeup:

Use a medium brush to apply black face paint around the eyes, creating deep, hollow eye sockets. Blend the edges slightly outward to soften the transition between the black and white areas, giving a ghostly, gothic appearance.

3.Spider Web Forehead Design:

With a thin brush, carefully paint a spider web design across the forehead. Start at the center above the eyebrows and extend outward, creating symmetrical, intricate webbing that connects above the eyes.

Ensure the lines are fine and detailed, adding small connecting strands to enhance the web effect.

4.Nose and Lip Detail:

Paint a small black triangle on the tip of the nose to mimic a skeletal or bat-like appearance.

Apply black paint or dark lipstick to the lips, keeping the look bold and gothic.

5.Final Touches:

Add small black accents, such as dots or tiny spiders, around the eyes or near the web design to enhance the spooky theme.

Ensure all lines are crisp and well-defined, especially on the web and around the eyes.

6.Accessories:

Pair the face paint with a bat hair accessory and a spider-themed costume, complete with web patterns or black lace to match the face design.

Gothic earrings, such as small pumpkins or spiders, add an extra touch of Halloween flair.

7.Tips:

Focus on the symmetry of the web design and the black eye makeup to create a balanced and polished look.

Keep the black and white contrast sharp to maintain the gothic, haunting appearance.

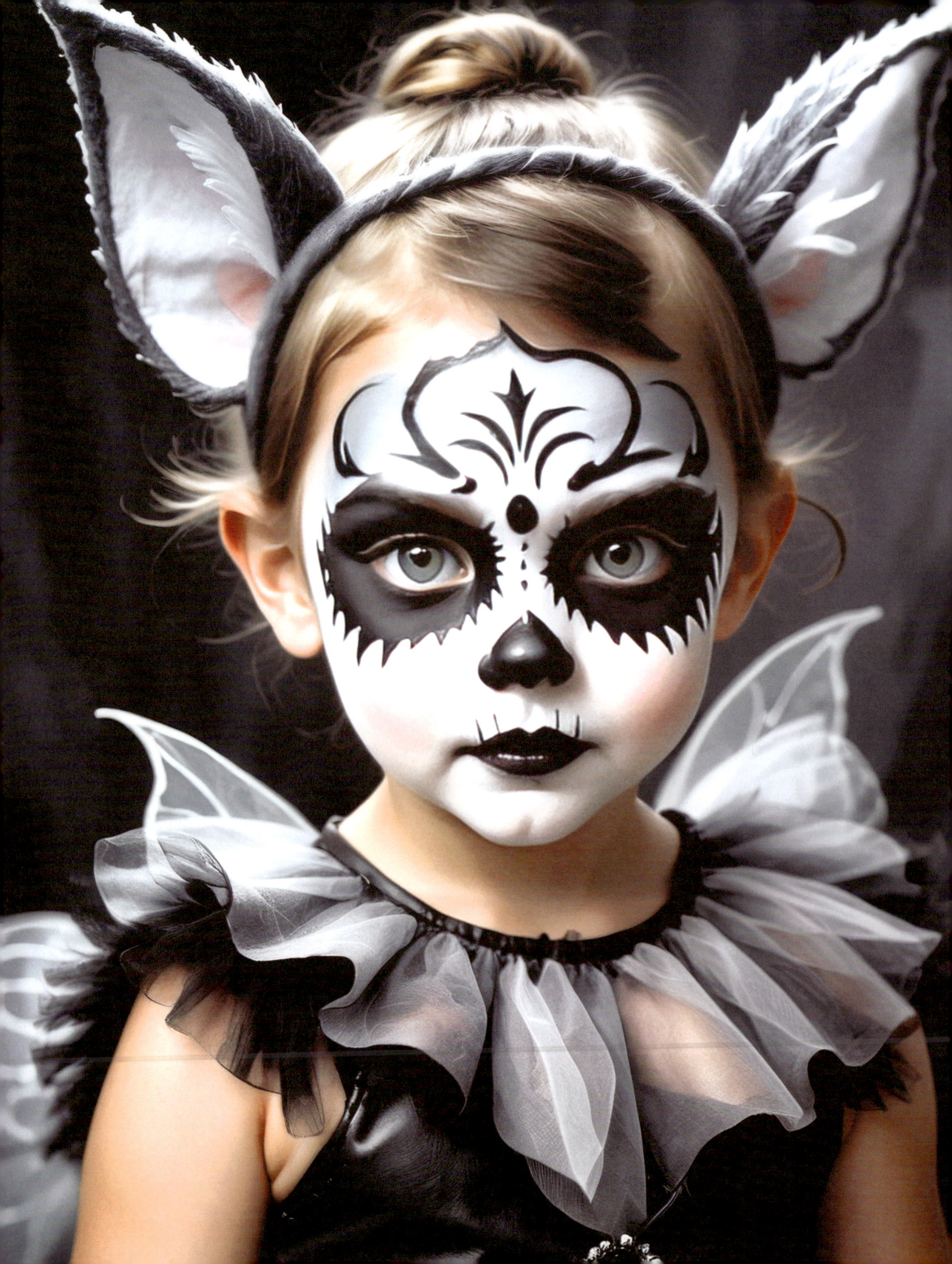

Dark Woodland Creature

Materials:

- Face paints: white, black

- Sponge, thin and medium brushes

- Optional: animal ear headband, dark or gothic-themed costume with ruffles

Steps:

1.White Base:

Apply a smooth, even layer of white face paint over the entire face using a sponge. This creates the base for the creature-like appearance.

2.Black Eye and Forehead Design:

Use a medium brush to apply black face paint around the eyes, extending outward to create a dramatic, mask-like effect. Blend slightly at the edges to soften the transition between the black and white.

With a thin brush, paint a detailed black design on the forehead, resembling a crown or ornate pattern that adds to the mystical and gothic theme.

3.Nose and Lip Details:

Paint the tip of the nose black, extending slightly down towards the lips to mimic an animal's snout.

Apply black face paint to the lips, and add small vertical lines from the lips to the chin to imitate the look of stitches or whiskers.

4.Cheek Accents:

Add sharp, triangular shapes extending from the black eye makeup towards the cheeks, giving the face a more angular and fierce appearance.

Ensure symmetry between both sides for a balanced look.

5.Final Touches:

Add small black dots above the lips or along the nose for additional detailing.

Double-check that all lines are clean and sharp, especially the black details around the eyes and forehead.

6.Accessories:

Complete the look with a headband featuring animal ears that match the face paint theme, such as wolf or bat ears.

Pair with a dark or gothic-themed costume, such as a dress with ruffles or lace, to enhance the overall appearance.

7.Tips:

Focus on the symmetry of the eye and forehead designs to create a cohesive and striking look.

Keep the black and white contrast bold and crisp to maintain the gothic, mysterious vibe.

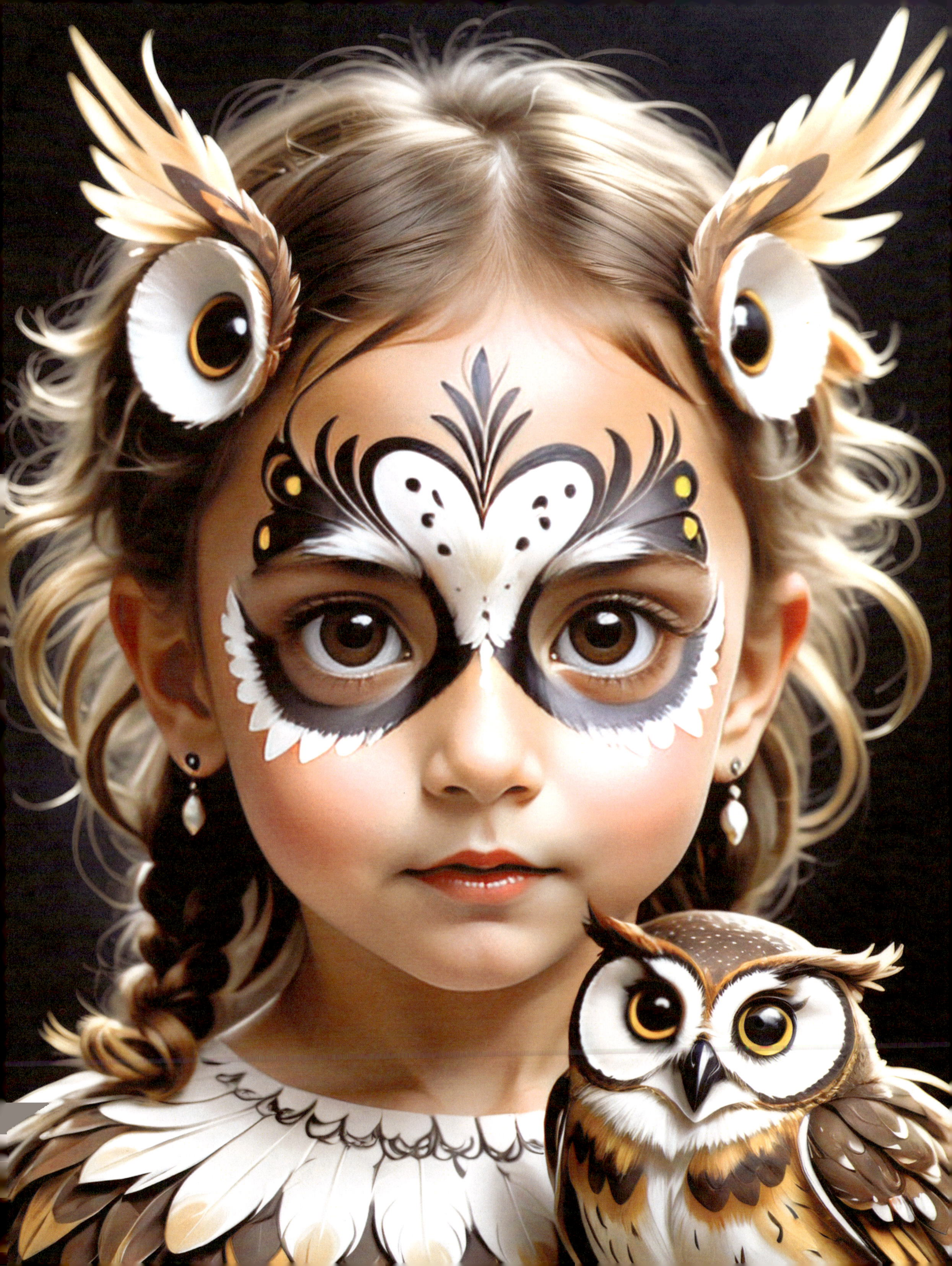

Owl Spirit

Materials:

- Face paints: white, brown, black, yellow

- Sponge, thin and medium brushes

- Optional: feathered hair accessories, owl-themed costume

Steps:

1.White Base and Eye Mask:

Start by applying a white base around the eyes using a sponge. Extend the white paint outward in a winged shape to mimic an owl's facial markings.

2.Brown and Black Feathers:

With a medium brush, apply brown paint around the white base, blending it to create the effect of feathers.

Use black paint to add details and outlines, focusing on creating small feather-like strokes around the edges of the white base.

3.Forehead Design:

With a thin brush, paint a decorative design on the forehead, resembling the shape of an owl's beak or feathers. Use a mix of black, brown, and white to add depth and texture.

Add small yellow dots or highlights to represent the bright eyes of an owl.

4.Cheek and Nose Accents:

Extend the feather design down to the cheeks, adding black and brown details to continue the owl-like pattern.

Paint a small black triangle on the nose to mimic an owl's beak.

5.Final Touches:

Ensure all lines are smooth and well-blended, particularly around the eyes and cheeks, to create a realistic feathered effect.

Add any additional details, like small white dots or feather highlights, to enhance the texture and depth.

6.Accessories:

Complete the look with feathered hair accessories, placed around the head to mimic owl ears or plumage.

Pair the face paint with an owl-themed costume, focusing on brown and white colors with feather patterns, to fully embody the owl spirit.

7.Tips:

Focus on blending the colors smoothly to create a realistic feather effect.

Keep the symmetry, especially around the eyes and forehead, to maintain a cohesive and polished look.

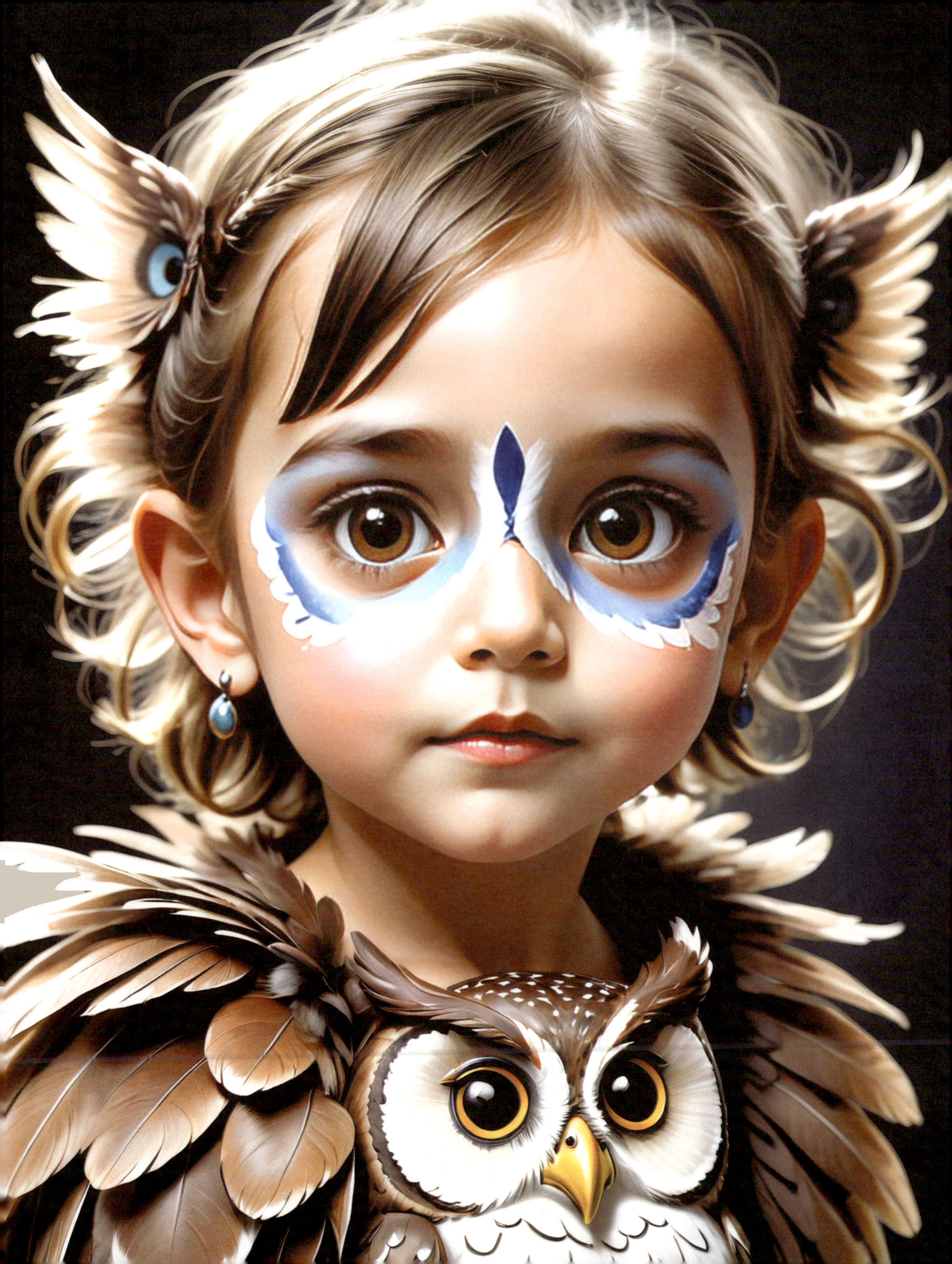

Mystical Owl Child

Materials:

- Face paints: white, blue, black, brown

- Sponge, thin and medium brushes

- Optional: owl feather hair accessories, owl-themed costume

Steps:

1.Blue and White Eye Mask:

Start by applying a blue base around the eyes using a medium brush. Create a winged shape extending outward from the eyes to mimic an owl's facial feathers.

Use white paint to add feather-like strokes around the edges of the blue base, blending softly into the blue to create a layered feather effect.

2.Brown and Black Feather Details:

With a thin brush, add brown and black strokes along the edges of the white feathers to give depth and texture. This will make the feathers look more realistic and layered.

Focus on creating fine lines to mimic the appearance of delicate feathers.

3.Forehead Accent:

Paint a small, delicate feather design on the center of the forehead using a mix of blue and white paint. This design should align with the eye mask, giving the face a cohesive, owl-inspired look.

4.Cheek and Nose Accents:

Use white paint to add small feather details extending from the eye mask down towards the cheeks.

Paint a small black triangle on the nose to represent an owl's beak, ensuring it aligns with the overall design.

5.Final Touches:

Ensure all feather lines are smooth and well-blended, particularly around the eyes and cheeks, to create a natural, feathered effect.

Add any additional small details, like dots or highlights, to enhance the texture and realism of the feathers.

6.Accessories:

Complete the look with feathered hair accessories styled like owl feathers or wings.

Pair the face paint with an owl-themed costume, featuring feather patterns or earthy tones to fully embody the forest owl theme.

7.Tips:

Focus on blending the blue and white colors smoothly to create a realistic feather effect.

Keep the feather details symmetrical to maintain a balanced and polished appearance.

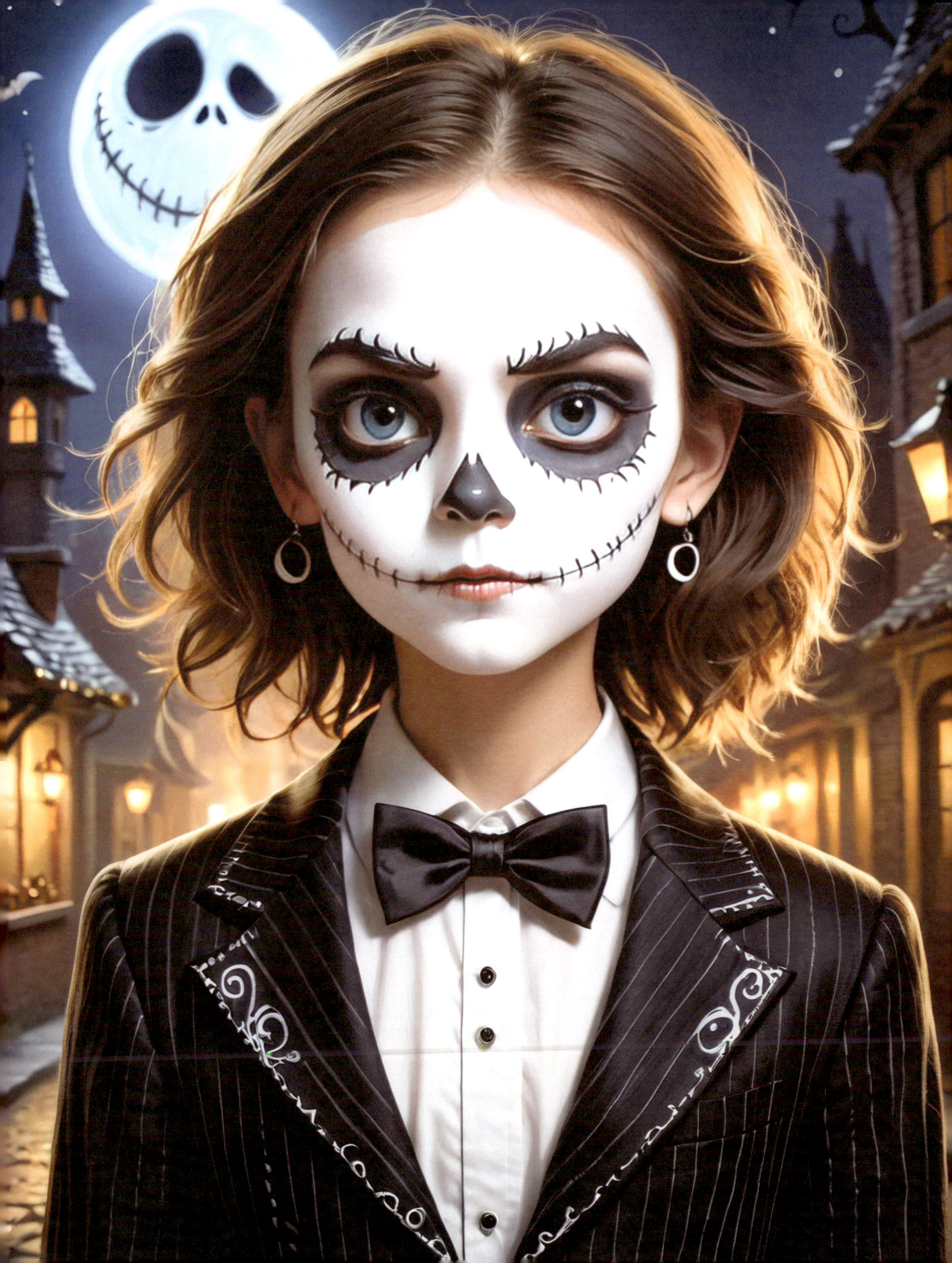

Skeleton Elegance

Materials:

- Face paints: white, black

- Sponge, thin and medium brushes

- Optional: black suit with pinstripes, bow tie

Steps:

1.White Base:

Apply a smooth, even layer of white face paint over the entire face using a sponge. This creates the skeletal base for the look.

2.Black Eye Sockets:

Use a medium brush to apply black face paint around the eyes, covering the eyelids and extending out slightly to create large, hollow eye sockets.

Blend the edges slightly to soften the transition between the black and white areas.

3.Nose and Mouth Details:

Paint a small black triangle or teardrop shape on the nose to mimic the hollow appearance of a skull.

For the mouth, use a thin brush to draw black lines extending from the corners of the mouth towards the cheeks, mimicking the look of skeletal teeth. Add vertical lines along the lips to complete the effect.

4.Forehead and Cheek Accents:

Use black paint to add thin, delicate lines on the forehead and along the cheekbones, enhancing the skeletal appearance. These can be subtle and should follow the natural contours of the face.

5.Final Touches:

Ensure all lines are crisp and well-defined, particularly around the eyes and mouth. Add any additional small details, like cracks or shading, to enhance the 3D effect of the skull.

6.Accessories:

Complete the look with a black suit, preferably with pinstripes, and a black bow tie to match the elegant, yet haunting theme.

Consider adding small, subtle accessories like black or silver earrings to complement the skeletal look.

7.Tips:

Focus on symmetry, especially with the eye sockets and mouth details, to create a balanced and polished appearance.

Keep the black and white contrast sharp to maintain the clean, sophisticated look of the skeleton.

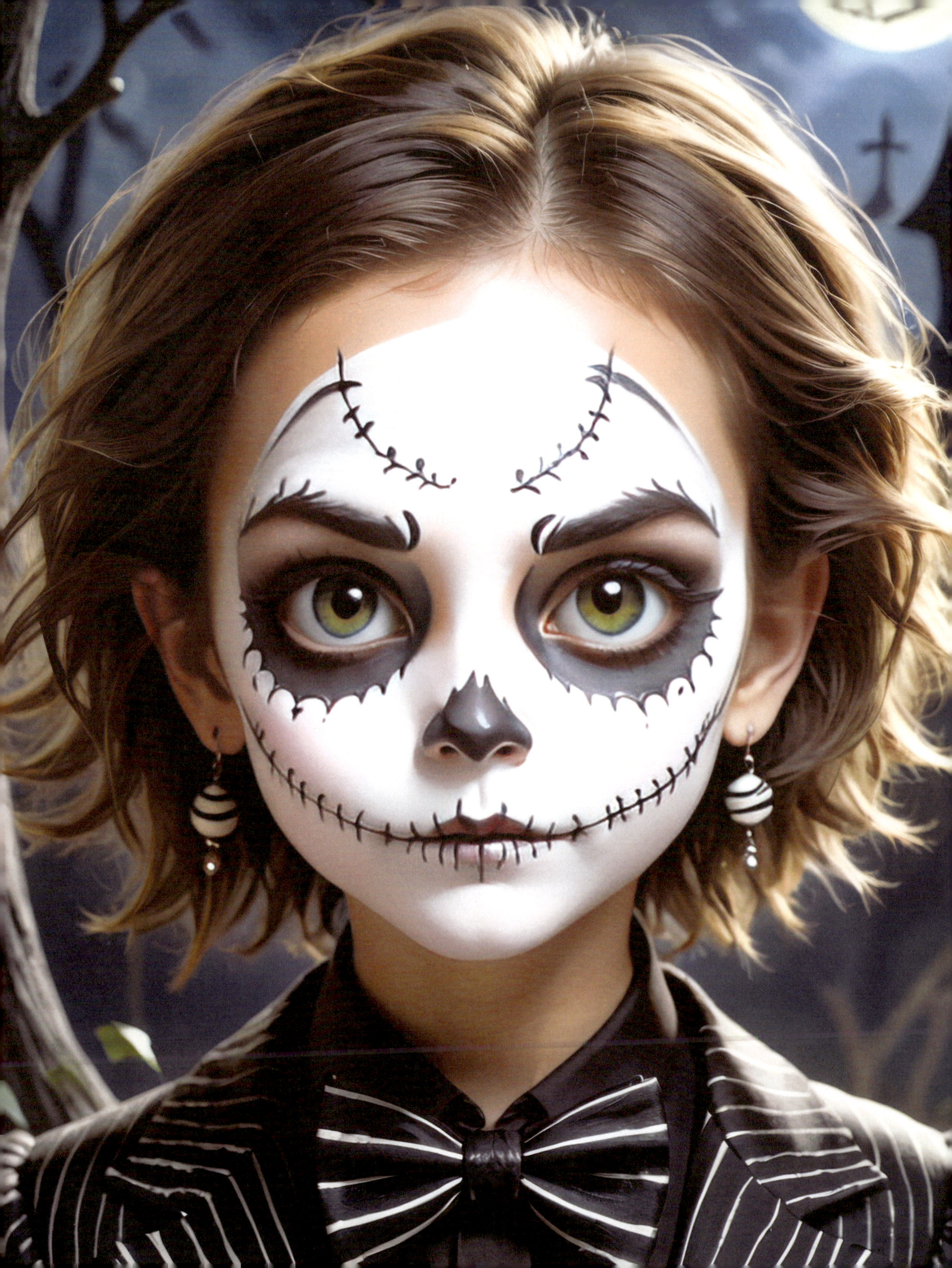

Stitched Skull

Materials:

- Face paints: white, black

- Sponge, thin and medium brushes

- Optional: black suit with pinstripes, striped bow tie, and matching earrings

Steps:

1.White Base:

Apply a smooth, even layer of white face paint over the entire face using a sponge. This will serve as the skeletal foundation for the look.

2.Black Eye Sockets:

Use a medium brush to apply black face paint around the eyes, covering the eyelids and extending outward to create large, hollow eye sockets. Blend the edges softly to give a sunken effect.

3.Stitches and Forehead Details:

With a thin brush, paint small black stitches across the forehead, following a curved line to mimic the look of a stitched seam. Extend these lines downwards, creating additional stitching effects around the eyes or mouth.

4.Nose and Mouth Details:

Paint a small black triangle or teardrop shape on the nose to mimic the hollow appearance of a skull.

For the mouth, use a thin brush to draw black lines extending from the corners of the mouth towards the cheeks, creating a stitched mouth effect. Add vertical lines along the lips and connecting to the horizontal lines for the look of sewn lips.

5.Final Touches:

Add small details like cracks or additional stitches along the forehead and cheeks to enhance the overall effect.

6.Accessories:

Complete the look with a black suit, preferably with pinstripes, and a striped bow tie to match the haunting theme.

Consider wearing earrings that match the stitching motif, such as black and white striped patterns, to add an extra touch of detail.

7.Tips:

Focus on the symmetry of the stitches and eye sockets to create a balanced and polished appearance.

Keep the black and white contrast strong to maintain the clean, spooky look of the skeleton.

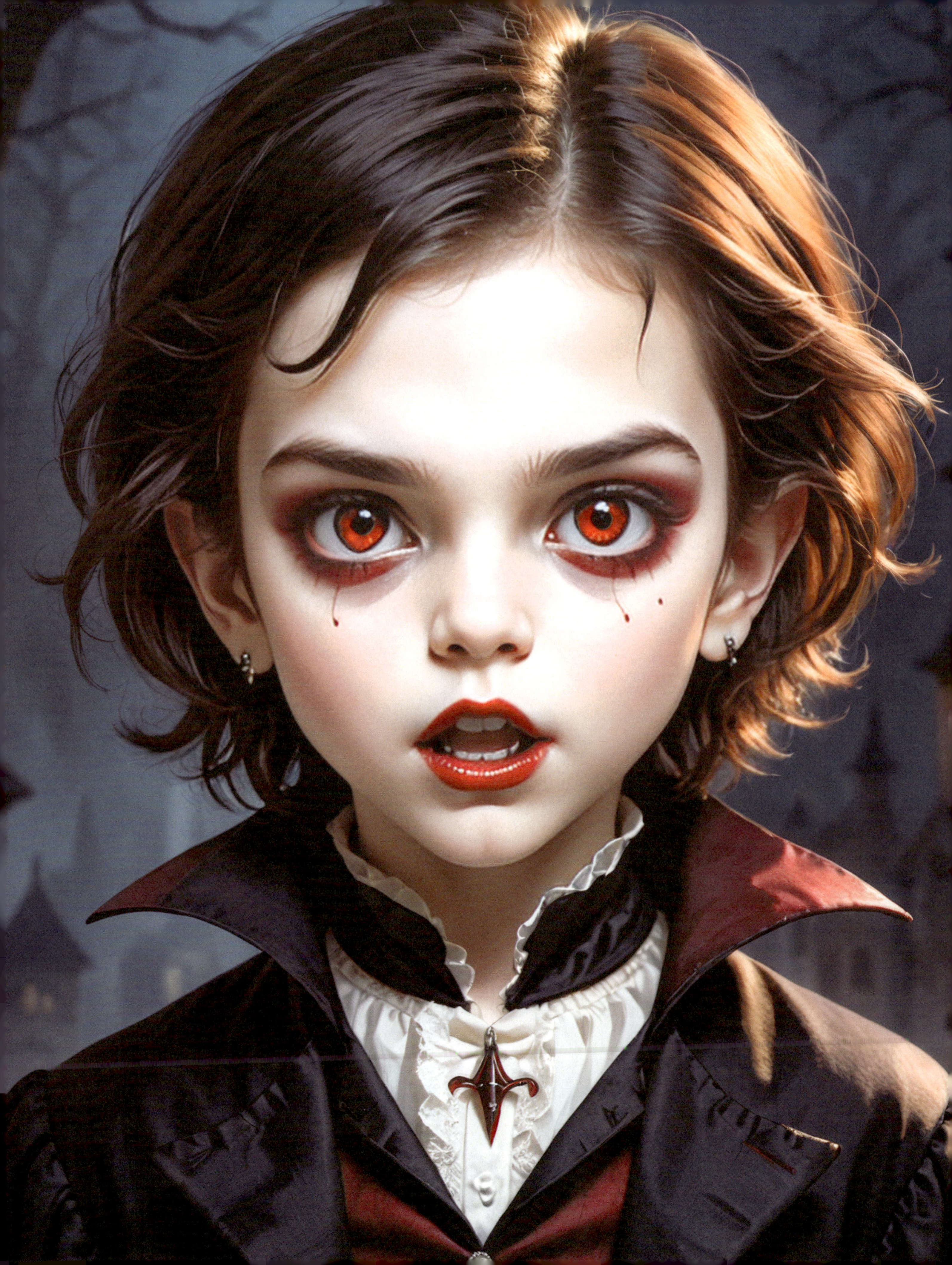

Little Vampire

Materials:

- Face paints: white, red, black

- Sponge, thin and medium brushes

- Optional: vampire costume with a high-collared cape and dark clothing

Steps:

1.Pale Base:

Apply a thin, even layer of white face paint over the entire face using a sponge. This creates the pale, undead look typical of a vampire.

2.Red Eyeshadow:

Use a medium brush to apply red face paint around the eyes, focusing on the eyelids and extending slightly outward for a dramatic effect. Blend the edges softly to give a shadowy, bloodshot look.

3.Black Eye Details:

Add black face paint just above the upper eyelids and along the lower lash line to intensify the eyes. Blend carefully to create depth without overpowering the red.

4.Blood Drips:

With a thin brush, paint small red lines extending downward from the lower lash line to mimic the appearance of blood tears. These should be subtle but noticeable.

5.Lip Color:

Apply red face paint to the lips, making sure to follow the natural lip shape. You can slightly extend the color beyond the edges for a fuller, more dramatic effect.

6.Final Touches:

Ensure all the lines and shadows are smooth and well-blended, especially around the eyes and lips, to maintain a polished look.

7.Accessories:

Complete the look with a classic vampire costume, featuring a high-collared cape, dark clothing, and possibly a brooch or pendant.

Consider styling the hair in a neat, slicked-back manner to enhance the aristocratic vampire image.

8.Tips:

Focus on blending the red and black around the eyes to create a smooth, shadowy effect.

Keep the blood drips subtle to maintain an elegant, rather than overly gory, appearance.

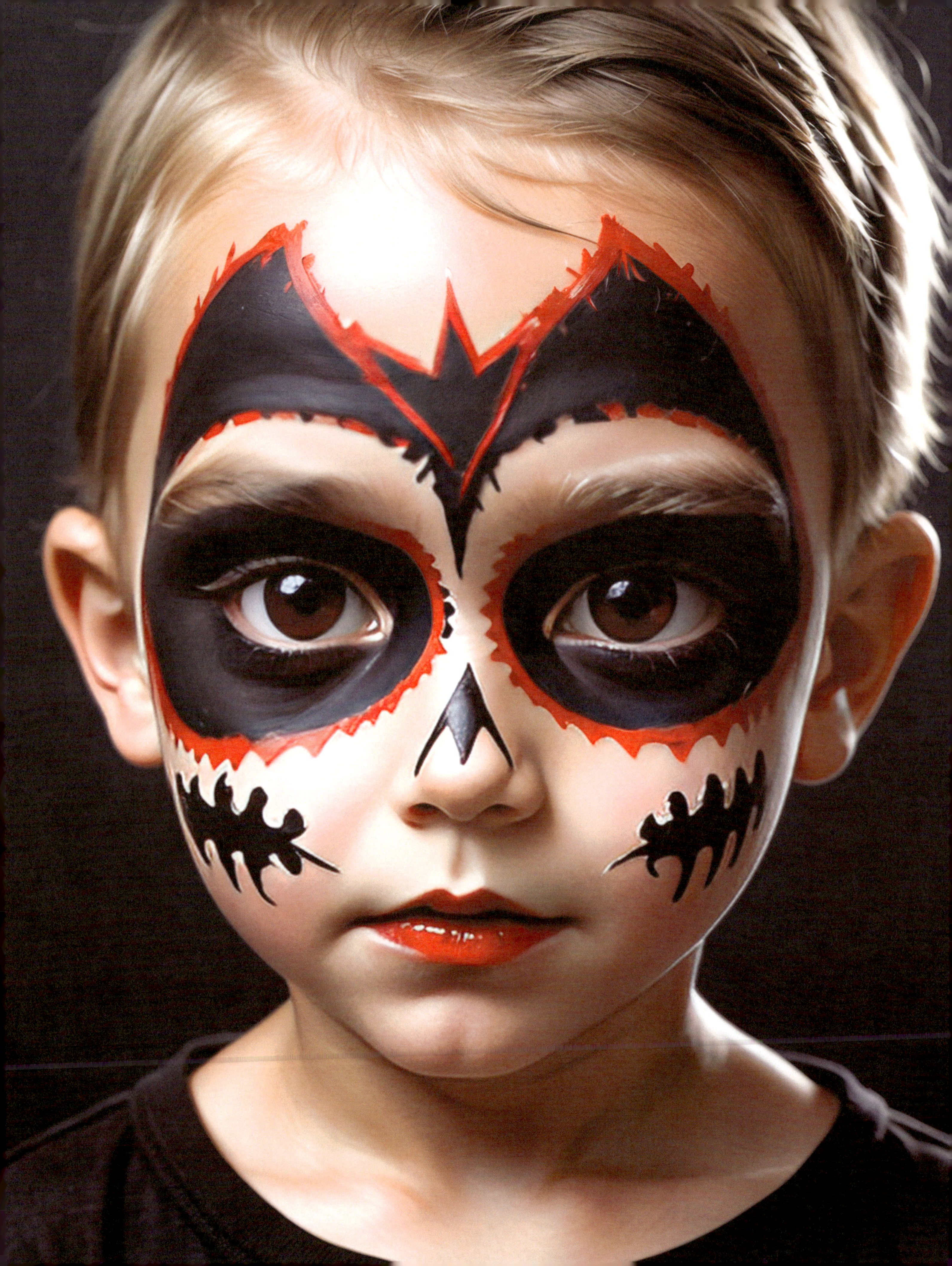

Dark Bat

Materials:

- Face paints: white, red, black

- Sponge, thin and medium brushes

- Optional: vampire costume with a high-collared cape and dark clothing

Steps:

1.Pale Base:

Apply a thin, even layer of white face paint over the entire face using a sponge. This creates the pale, undead look typical of a vampire.

2.Red Eyeshadow:

Use a medium brush to apply red face paint around the eyes, focusing on the eyelids and extending slightly outward for a dramatic effect. Blend the edges softly to give a shadowy, bloodshot look.

3.Black Eye Details:

Add black face paint just above the upper eyelids and along the lower lash line to intensify the eyes. Blend carefully to create depth without overpowering the red.

4.Blood Drips:

With a thin brush, paint small red lines extending downward from the lower lash line to mimic the appearance of blood tears. These should be subtle but noticeable.

5.Lip Color:

Apply red face paint to the lips, making sure to follow the natural lip shape. You can slightly extend the color beyond the edges for a fuller, more dramatic effect.

6.Final Touches:

Ensure all the lines and shadows are smooth and well-blended, especially around the eyes and lips, to maintain a polished look.

7.Accessories:

Complete the look with a classic vampire costume, featuring a high-collared cape, dark clothing, and possibly a brooch or pendant.

8.Tips:

Focus on blending the red and black around the eyes to create a smooth, shadowy effect.

Keep the blood drips subtle to maintain an elegant, rather than overly gory, appearance.

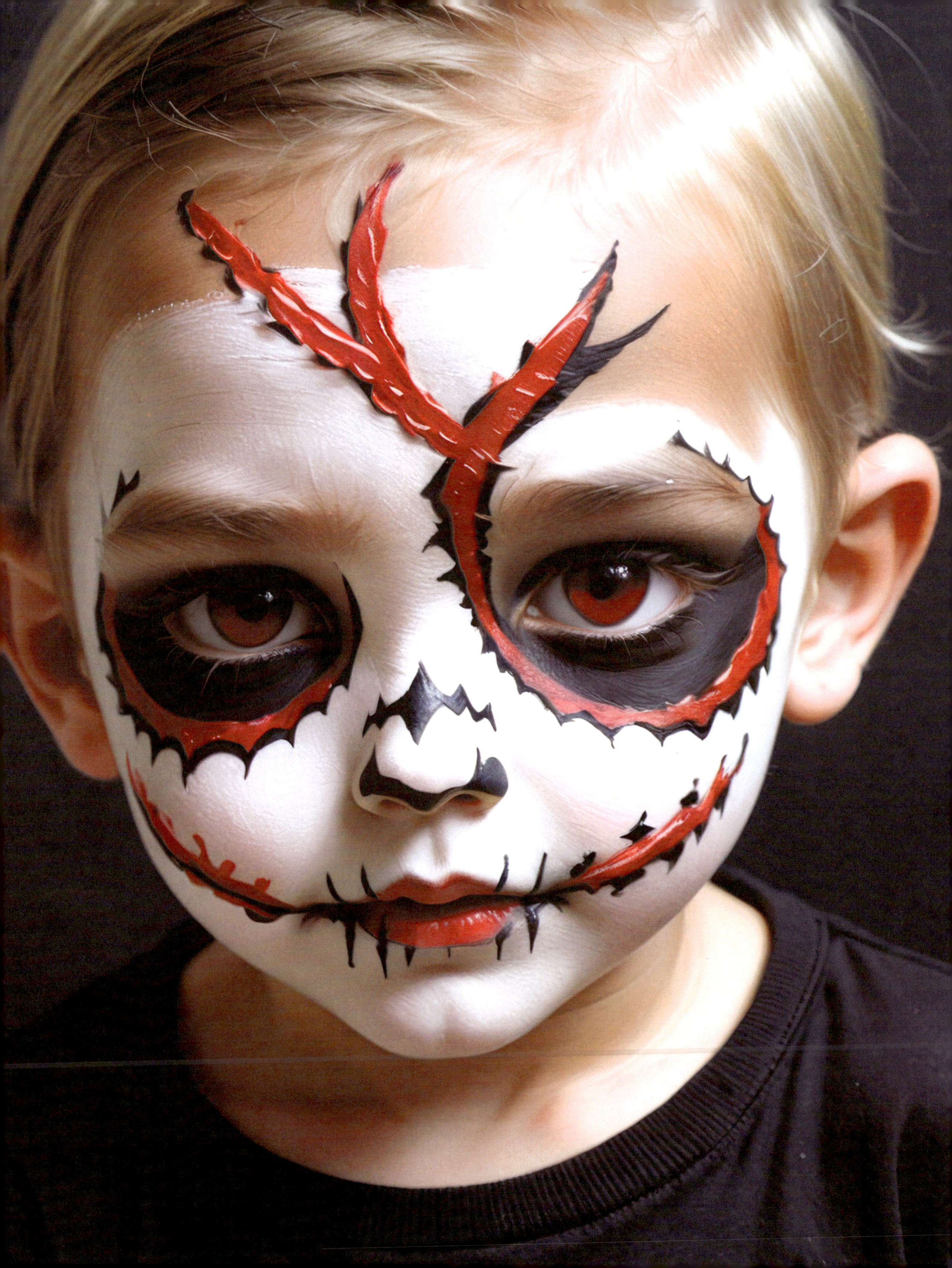

Stitched Horror

Materials:

- Face paints: white, black, red

- Sponge, thin and medium brushes

Steps:

1.White Base:

Apply a smooth, even layer of white face paint over the entire face using a sponge. This sets the stage for the stitched effect.

2.Black Eye Circles:

Use a medium brush to paint large, black circles around the eyes, creating a hollowed-out effect. Make sure the edges are clean and rounded.

3.Red and Black Stitches:

With a thin brush, outline the eye circles with red paint, adding jagged edges to mimic torn flesh.

Add black stitches around the mouth and eyes, crossing over the red outline to create a creepy, sewn-together look.

4.Forehead Gash:

Paint a red, jagged gash on the forehead with a thin brush. Add black details along the edges of the gash to give it depth and make it appear as if the skin is torn.

5.Lip Color:

Apply red face paint to the lips, following the natural shape but adding a slight sharpness to the edges to enhance the stitched-together look.

6,Final Touches:

Ensure all the lines are sharp and well-defined, particularly the stitches and gash. Make sure the red and black contrast sharply against the white base.

7.Tips:

Focus on making the stitches look realistic by varying the length and thickness.

Keep the gash on the forehead jagged and uneven to enhance the horror effect.

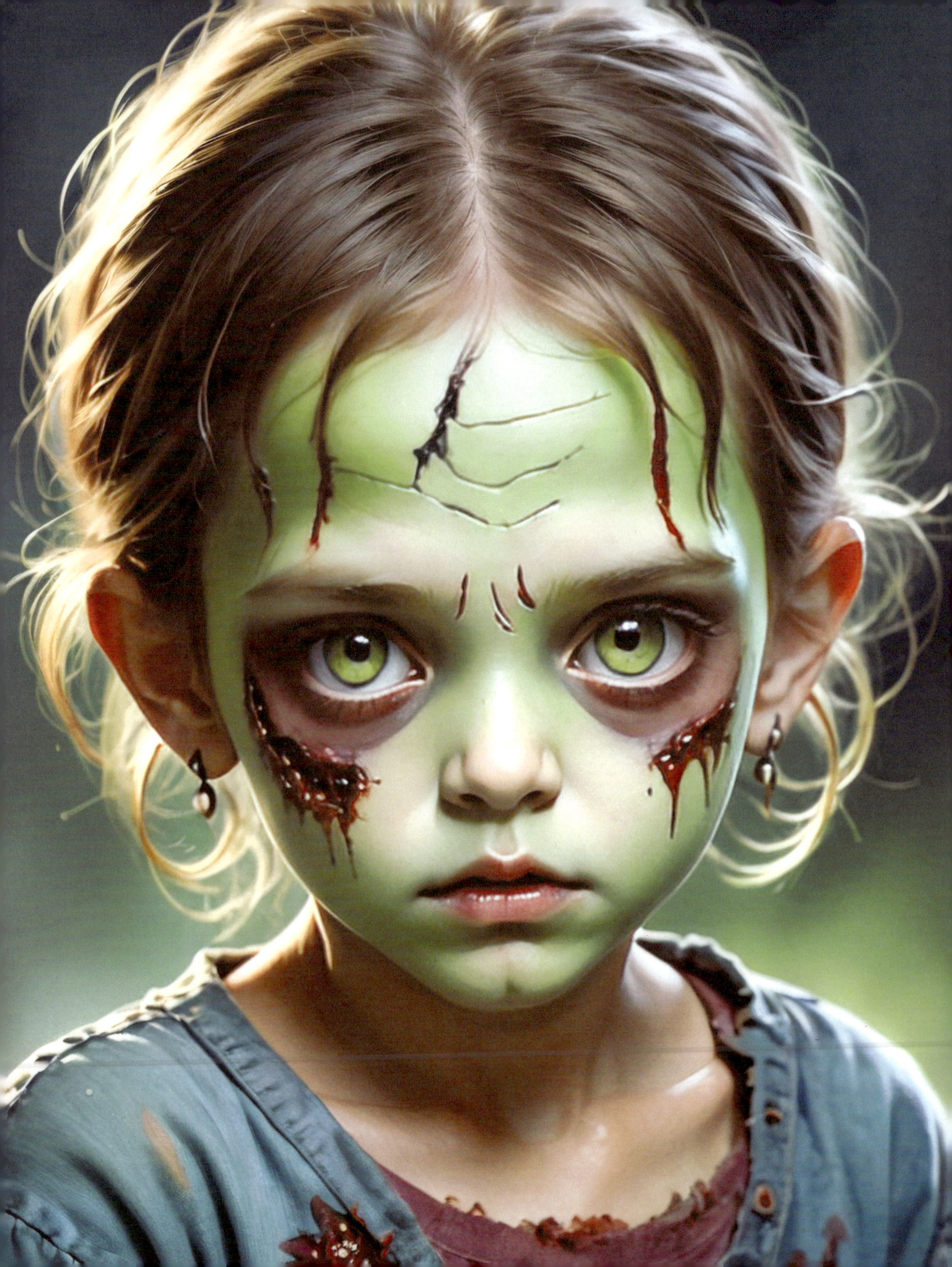

Little Zombie

Materials:

- Face paints: green, black, red, dark purple

- Sponge, thin and medium brushes

Optional: costume with torn and tattered clothing

Steps:

1.Green Base:

Start by applying a green face paint base all over the face using a sponge. Ensure the coverage is smooth and even, creating a sickly, undead appearance.

2.Dark Eye Circles:

Use a medium brush to apply dark purple or black paint around the eyes, blending it outward to create sunken, tired eyes typical of a zombie. This will give a gaunt, haunted look.

3.Bloody Wounds:

With a thin brush, paint small wounds on the forehead and cheeks using red face paint. Add black or dark purple around the edges of the wounds to give them depth.

Add dripping blood effects from the wounds by extending the red paint downwards, creating the illusion of fresh, bleeding cuts.

4.Cracks and Scars:

Use black face paint to draw thin cracks and scars on the forehead and cheeks, mimicking the appearance of decaying skin. These can be random, jagged lines that add to the overall creepy effect.

5.Highlighting and Shading:

Add shading around the eyes, cheekbones, and jawline with a darker green or purple to enhance the hollow, skeletal look.

Use a lighter green or even white to highlight areas like the nose bridge and chin to create contrast and make the face appear more dimensional.

6.Final Touches:

Add any additional details such as small blood splatters or more scars to enhance the overall zombie effect.

Ensure the wounds look realistic by blending the edges into the green base and adding small touches of dark colors around them.

7.Tips:

Use a light hand when adding the darker colors to avoid overwhelming the green base, which is essential for the undead look.

The key to a convincing zombie look is the combination of sickly green skin with realistic wounds and shadows, so take your time blending the colors.

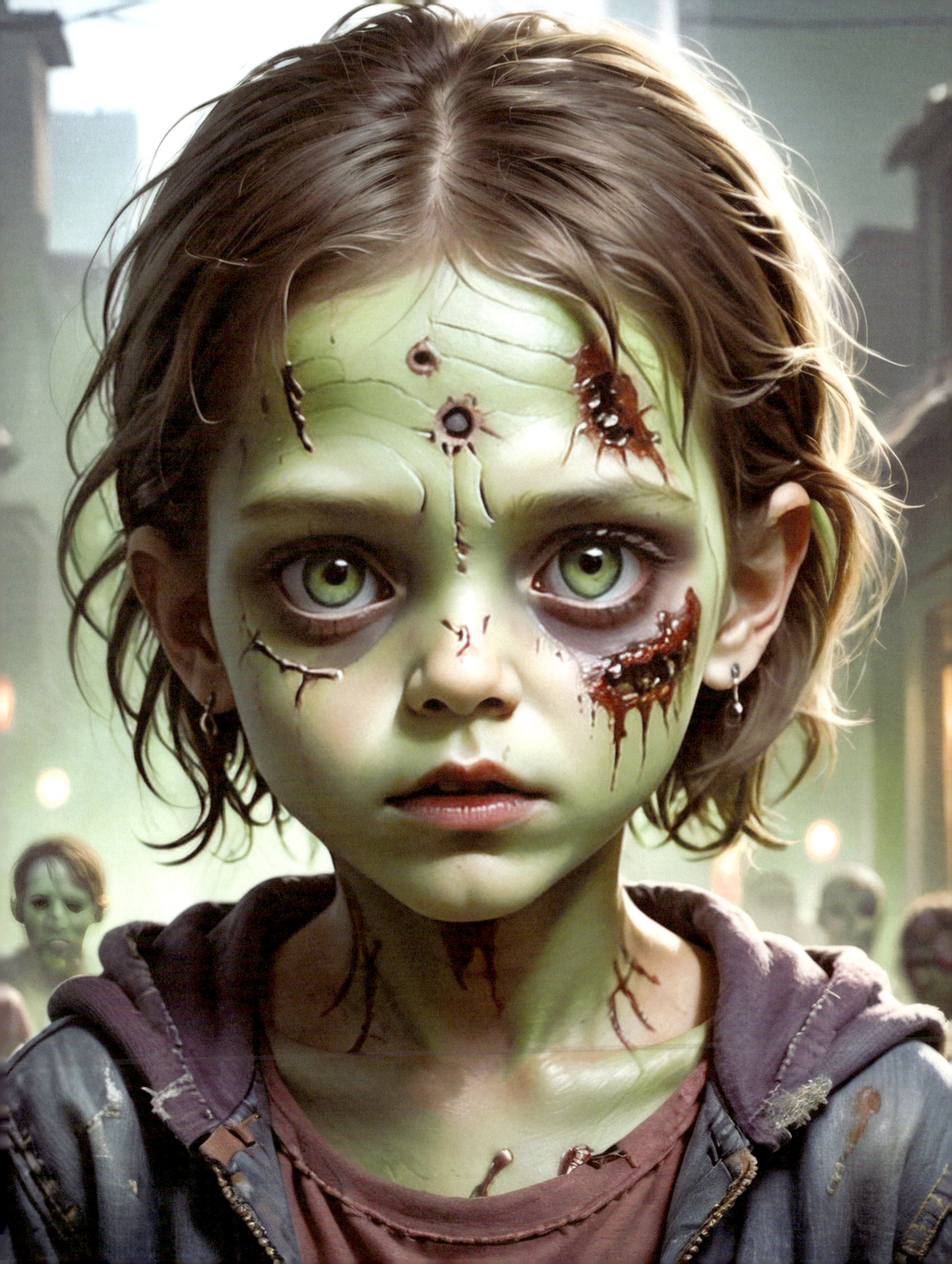

Urban Zombie

Materials:

- Face paints: green, black, red, dark purple

- Sponge, thin and medium brushes

Steps:

1.Green Base:

Apply a green face paint base all over the face using a sponge. This should create an even, sickly green complexion that forms the foundation of the zombie look.

2.Sunken Eyes:

Use a medium brush to apply dark purple or black paint around the eyes, blending outward to create a sunken, tired appearance typical of a zombie. Extend this shading slightly downward and outward to enhance the gaunt look.

3.Wounds and Bullet Holes:

With a thin brush, create realistic wounds and bullet holes on the forehead and cheeks using red face paint. Add depth to the wounds by outlining them with dark purple or black.

To create the bullet hole effect, use black paint for the center, then add red around it to mimic blood. Add highlights with white to give a more three-dimensional appearance.

4.Blood Effects:

Add dripping blood effects from the wounds by using a thin brush with red paint. Let the paint streak downward from the wounds, mimicking the effect of blood slowly trickling down the face.

Add some smeared blood effects around the mouth or other areas to suggest recent feeding or injury.

5.Cracks and Veins:

Use black face paint to draw thin cracks and veins across the forehead, cheeks, and neck. These should be irregular and jagged, mimicking the appearance of decaying skin or infection spreading beneath the surface.

You can also add small green or brown veins to enhance the infected look.

6.Shading and Contouring:

Add shading around the face with darker green or purple paint, particularly around the cheekbones, temples, and neck. This will make the face appear more hollow and skeletal.

Use lighter green or white paint to highlight areas like the nose, chin, and forehead, creating contrast and making the wounds stand out more.

7.Tips:

The key to a realistic zombie look is in the details. Take your time adding small cracks, veins, and realistic blood effects to make the face appear as decayed and eerie as possible.

Blend the colors well, especially around the wounds, to ensure they look like they are part of the skin rather than painted on top.

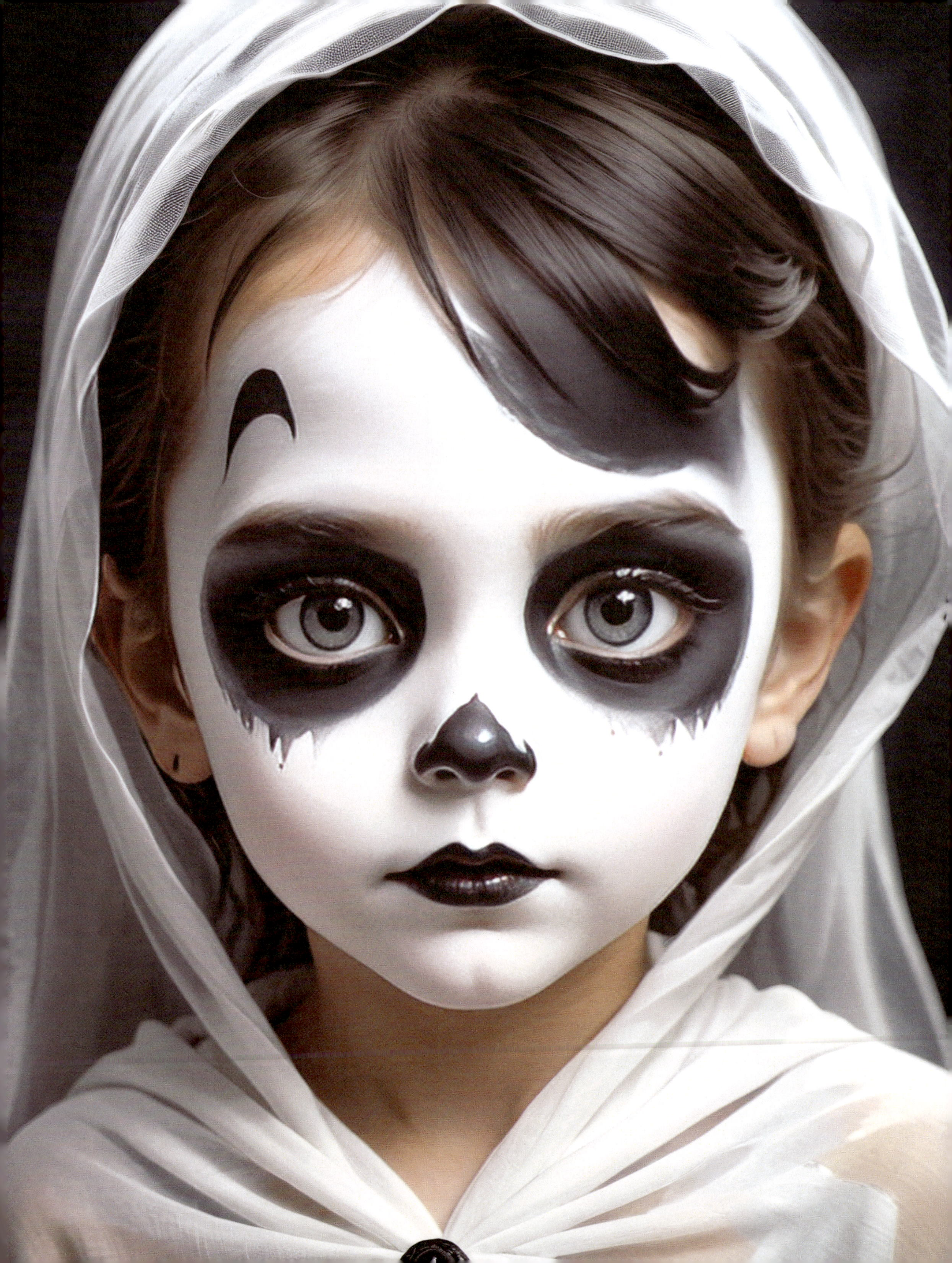

Ghostly Elegance

Materials:

- Face paints: white, black

- Sponge, thin and medium brushes

- Optional: white or light-colored veil, ghostly costume

Steps:

1.White Base:

Start by applying a smooth, even layer of white face paint over the entire face using a sponge. This will create the ghostly, ethereal look that serves as the foundation for the design.

2.Black Eye Circles:

With a medium brush, apply black face paint around the eyes, extending slightly outward to create hollow, sunken eyes. Blend the black paint softly to avoid harsh lines, giving a more haunting appearance.

3.Nose and Lip Details:

Paint a small black triangle on the tip of the nose, keeping the lines sharp to mimic a skeletal nose.

Apply black paint or dark lipstick to the lips, making sure the coverage is even and the lines are clean.

4.Forehead Accent:

Paint a simple, curved black line on the forehead to add a subtle but eerie detail that enhances the ghostly theme.

This detail can be minimalist, as the focus should remain on the eyes and the overall pale appearance.

5.Final Touches:

Add any additional black shading around the face, such as under the cheekbones or along the jawline, to enhance the skeletal, ghostly appearance.

Ensure all edges and lines are smooth and blended to maintain the soft, haunting look.

6.Accessories:

Complete the look with a light-colored or white veil draped over the head and shoulders, creating a phantom-like silhouette.

7.Tips:

The key to this look is in the subtle blending of the black and white paints to create a soft, ghostly effect.

Focus on keeping the lines clean and the overall look minimalist to maintain the haunting, elegant aesthetic.

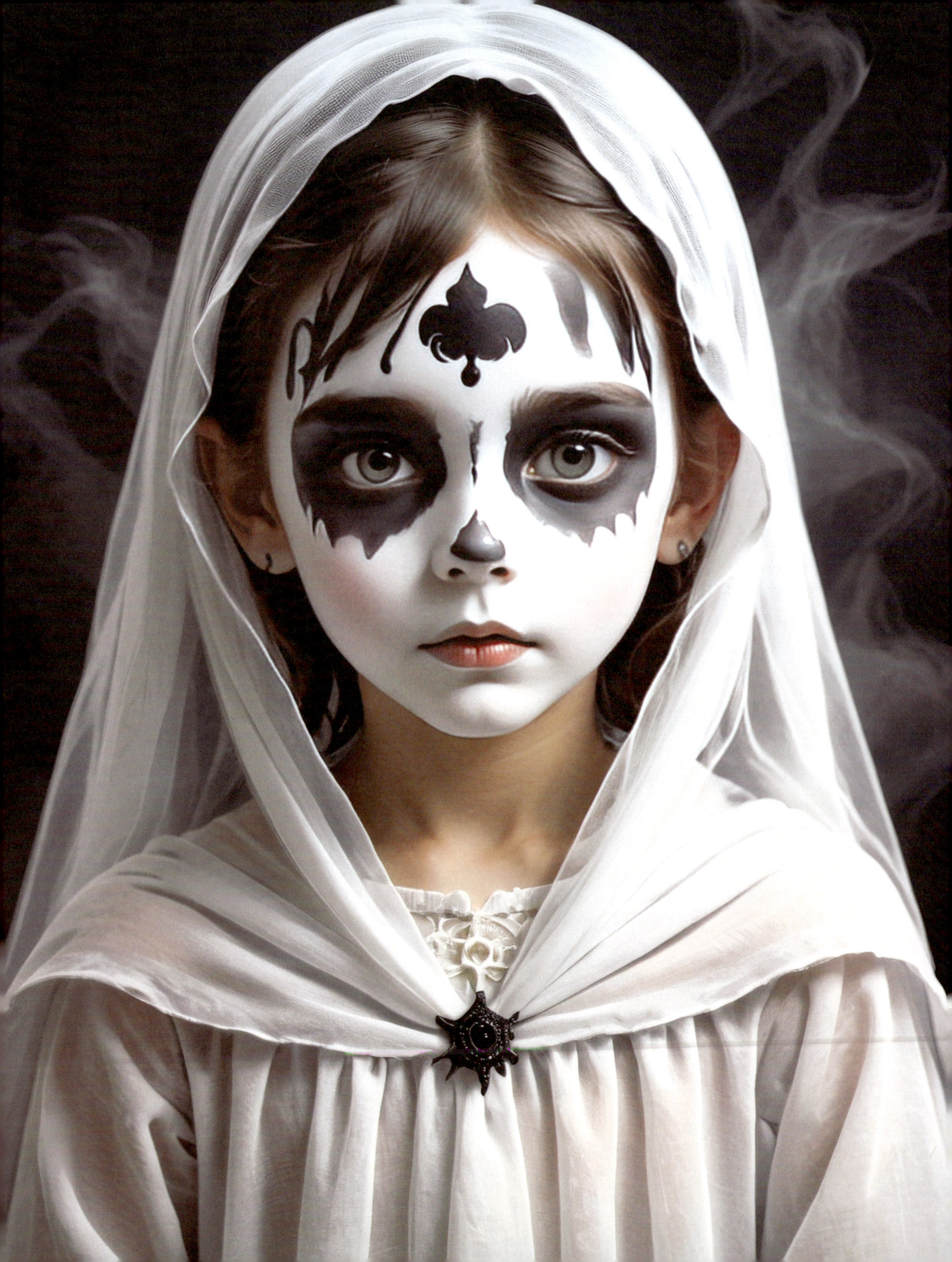

Ethereal Spirit

Materials:

- Face paints: white, black

- Sponge, thin and medium brushes

- Optional: white veil, ghostly costume with a dark brooch or clasp

Steps:

1.White Base:

Apply a smooth, even layer of white face paint over the entire face using a sponge to create a pale, ghostly complexion.

2.Black Eye Makeup:

Use a medium brush to apply black paint around the eyes, creating hollow, sunken sockets. Blend the black outward softly to create a shadowed effect that extends slightly beyond the eye area.

Add subtle streaks or drips of black extending from the lower eyelids to enhance the eerie, haunted look.

3.Forehead Symbol:

With a thin brush, paint a black, gothic-style symbol or design in the center of the forehead. This could be a fleur-de-lis or similar intricate pattern that adds a touch of elegance and mystery.

4.Cheekbone and Chin Details:

Lightly outline the cheekbones and chin with black paint, blending it inward to create a more angular, skeletal appearance. These details should be subtle, adding depth without overpowering the overall look.

5.Nose and Lips:

Paint the tip of the nose black in a small triangle shape to mimic a skeletal nose.

Apply a minimal amount of black paint to the lips or leave them pale to maintain the ghostly appearance.

6.Final Touches:

Add any additional shading around the face with light grey or black to create depth, especially around the temples and jawline.

Ensure all lines are smooth and blended to keep the look elegant and haunting.

7.Accessories:

Complete the look with a sheer white veil draped over the head and shoulders, creating a phantom-like silhouette.

A ghostly costume with a dark brooch or clasp at the neck adds a striking contrast and enhances the ethereal quality of the look.

8.Tips:

Focus on blending the black and white paints smoothly to maintain a soft, haunting effect.

The symbol on the forehead should be centered and symmetrical to draw attention to the eyes and add a focal point to the design.

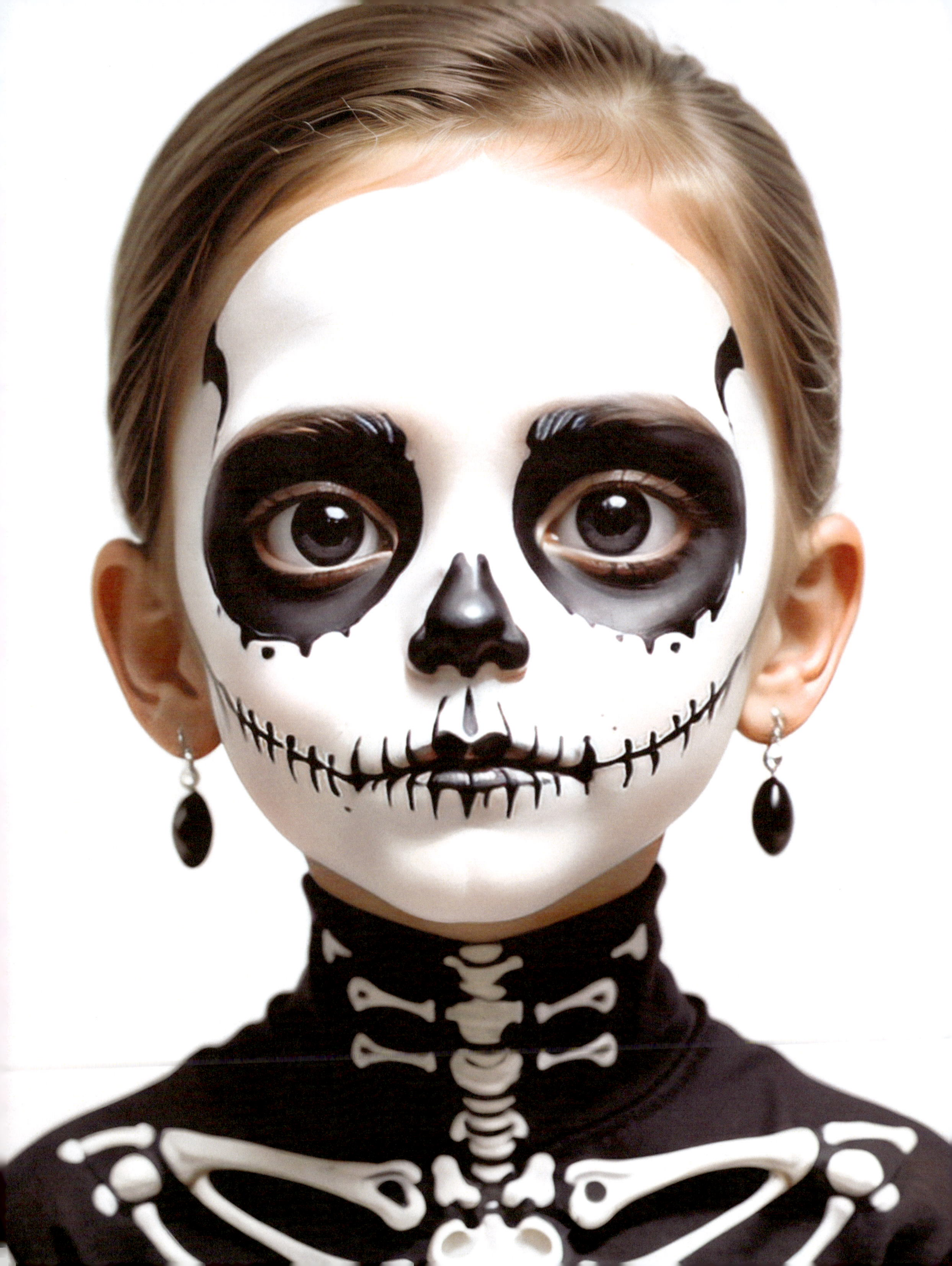

Classic Skeleton

Materials:

- Face paints: white, black

- Sponge, thin and medium brushes

- Optional: skeleton costume, black earrings

Steps:

1.White Base:

Apply a smooth, even layer of white face paint over the entire face using a sponge. This will serve as the base for the skeletal look.

2.Black Eye Sockets:

With a medium brush, apply black face paint around the eyes to create large, hollow eye sockets. Ensure the paint covers the area above the eyebrows and down to the upper cheeks, creating a rounded shape.

3.Nose Detail:

Paint the tip of the nose with black face paint in a small, inverted heart or teardrop shape to mimic the hollow nose of a skeleton.

4.Mouth and Teeth:

Using a thin brush, draw a black line across the lips, extending it outward to the cheeks. This line represents the jawline of the skeleton.

Add vertical lines along this horizontal line to create the appearance of teeth. The lines should vary in size, with longer lines at the center and shorter ones near the edges.

5.Forehead and Cheekbone Shading:

Add subtle black shading along the hairline, temples, and under the cheekbones to enhance the skeletal effect.

Blend these areas carefully to avoid stark lines, maintaining a smooth transition between the white base and black shading.

6.Final Touches:

Go over any areas that need more definition, such as the edges of the eye sockets or the teeth, to ensure the design is sharp and clean.

7.Accessories:

Pair the face paint with a skeleton costume to complete the look. Black earrings or simple accessories can enhance the elegant, yet spooky appearance.

8.Tips:

The key to this look is symmetry and smooth blending. Take your time to ensure both sides of the face are even and the black and white paints are well-blended.

Keep the lines for the teeth sharp and precise to maintain the classic skeletal look.

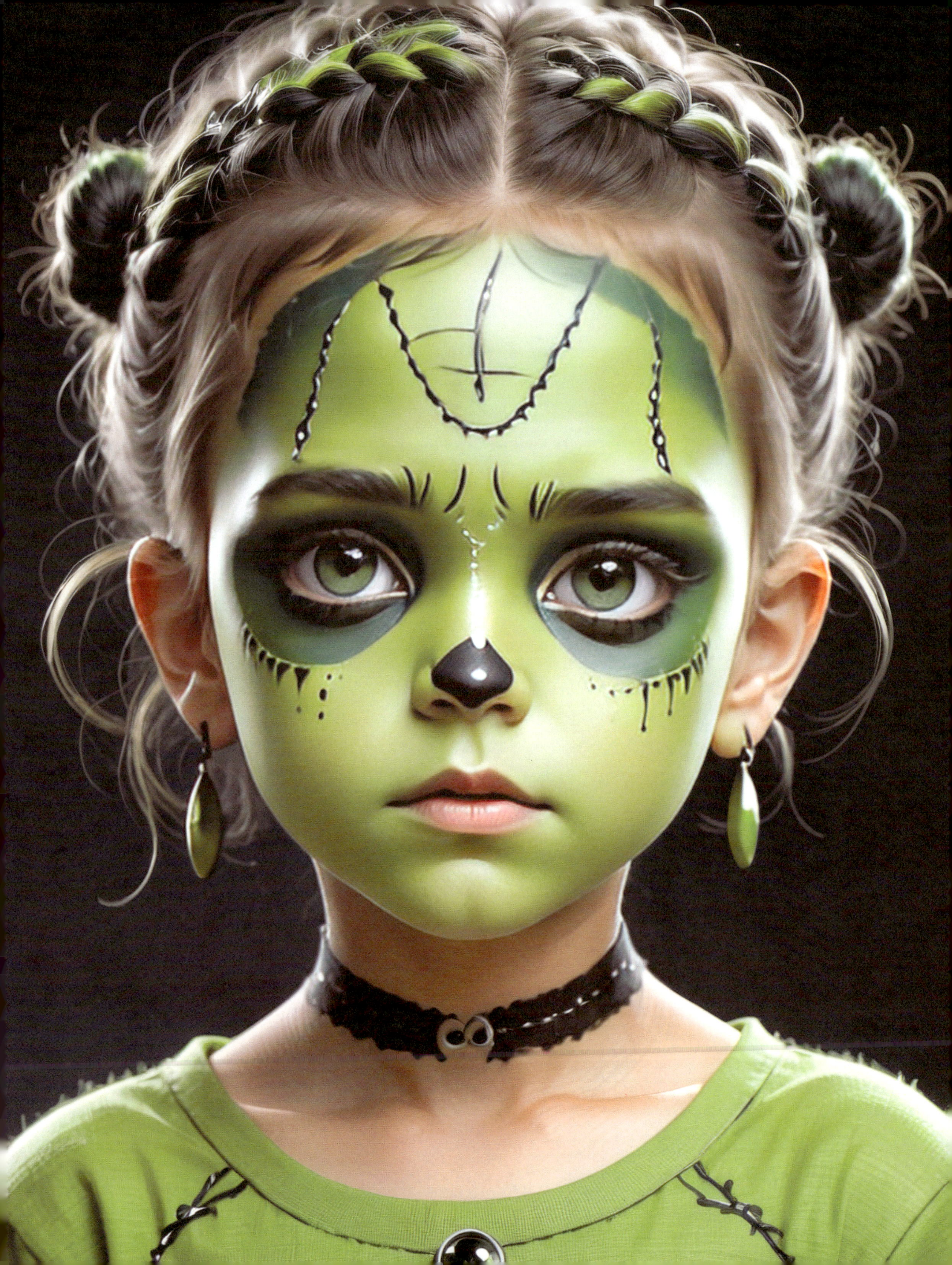

Green Ghoul

Materials:

- Face paints: green, black, white

- Sponge, thin and medium brushes

- Optional: green accessories, black choker, and matching earrings

Steps:

1.Green Base:

Apply a smooth, even layer of green face paint over the entire face using a sponge. This will serve as the base for the monster-like appearance.

2.Dark Eye Shading:

Use a medium brush to apply dark green or black paint around the eyes, creating a shadowed effect. Blend the edges to soften the transition between the green base and the darker eye areas.

3.Stitch Marks:

With a thin brush, use black face paint to create small, jagged stitch marks across the forehead, cheeks, and chin. These stitches should resemble those seen on Frankenstein's monster, giving the impression of a creature pieced together.

4.Nose and Lip Details:

Paint the tip of the nose with black face paint in a small, rounded triangle shape, similar to a cartoonish animal or monster nose.

Keep the lips subtle, with either a light green shade or leave them natural, to maintain focus on the eyes and stitches.

5.Forehead and Cheekbone Accents:

Add thin black lines on the forehead to resemble cracks or additional stitching, enhancing the stitched-together look.

6.Final Touches:

Add white highlights along the edges of the stitches and around the eyes to give a more three-dimensional appearance.

7.Accessories:

Pair the face paint with a black choker, green earrings, and other matching accessories to complete the look.

A hairstyle with small braids or buns, possibly with green accents, will enhance the theme and tie the entire look together.

8.Tips:

Focus on symmetry, especially when applying the stitches and shading, to create a balanced and cohesive design.

The use of white highlights is crucial for making the stitches and other details pop against the green base.

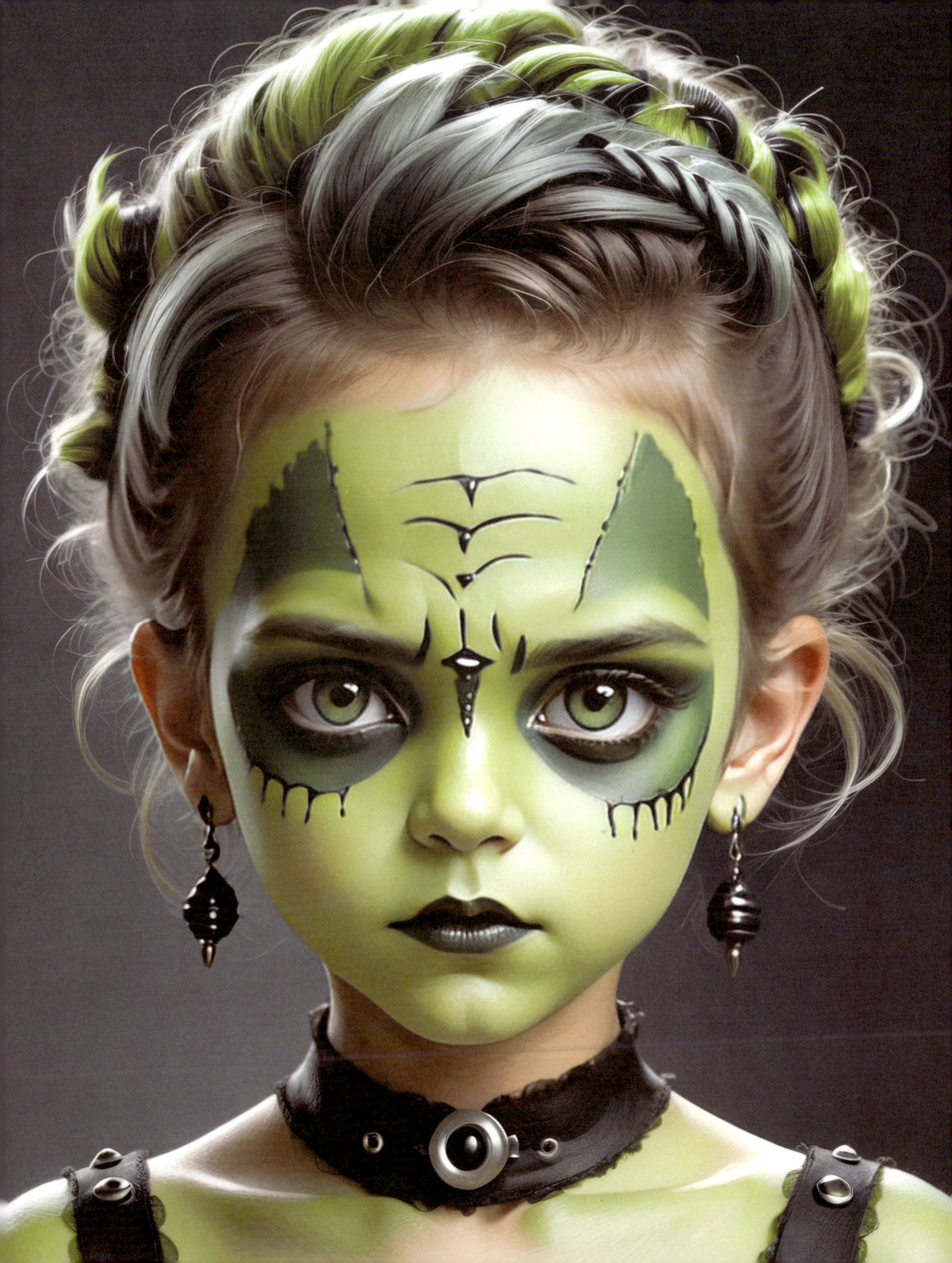

Gothic Green Monster

Materials:

- Face paints: green, black

- Sponge, thin and medium brushes

- Optional: black choker, gothic earrings, and accessories

Steps:

1.Green Base:

Apply a smooth, even layer of green face paint over the entire face using a sponge. This will serve as the base for the creature-like appearance.

2.Dark Eye Shading:

Use a medium brush to apply dark green or black paint around the eyes, focusing on creating deep shadows under the eyes. Blend the edges for a soft transition between the green base and the darker areas, giving a hollow, intense look.

3.Forehead and Cheekbone Details:

With a thin brush, use black face paint to create thin, jagged lines on the forehead, mimicking cracks or scars typical of a monster or Frankenstein's bride.

Add small, decorative lines or dots on the cheeks extending from the outer corners of the eyes to enhance the gothic, stitched-together look.

4.Nose and Lip Details:

Paint the tip of the nose with black face paint in a small, rounded triangle shape, keeping the lines sharp for a polished look.

Apply black paint or dark lipstick to the lips, maintaining the gothic and intense vibe of the character.

5.Final Touches:

Add subtle black shading along the jawline, temples, and under the cheekbones to create a more angular, sculpted appearance.

6.Hair Accents:

If possible, style the hair with green and black highlights or use temporary hair color to match the face paint. Braids or twists can add to the gothic and otherworldly appearance.

7.Accessories:

Pair the face paint with a black choker featuring metallic details, gothic earrings, and other matching accessories.

8.Tips:

Symmetry is key, especially when applying the stitches and shading, to create a balanced and cohesive design.

The use of black accents is crucial for making the features stand out against the green base, so take your time with these details.

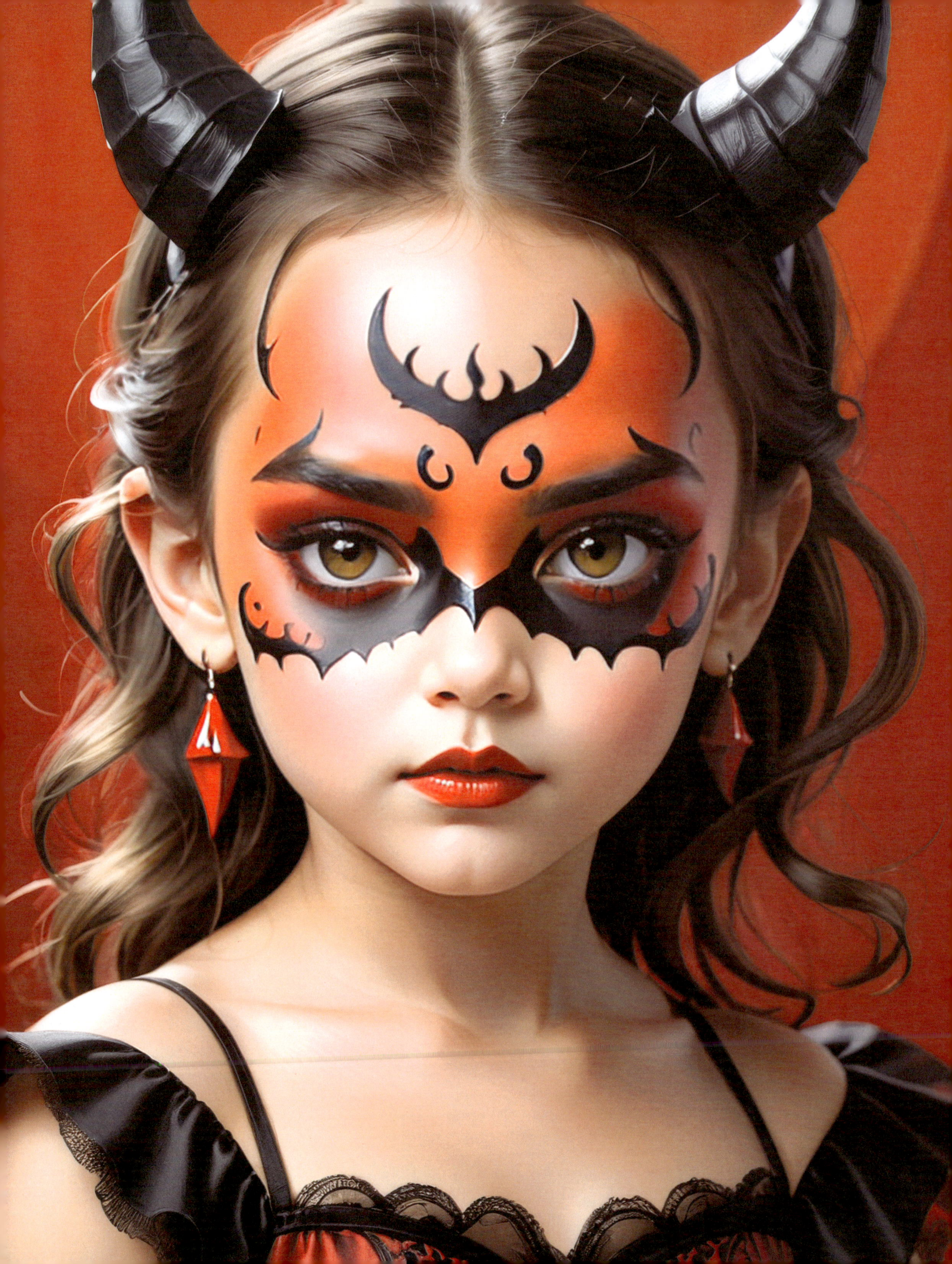

Little Devil

Materials:

- Face paints: red, black

- Sponge, thin and medium brushes

- Optional: devil horns headband, red earrings, and matching accessories

Steps:

1.Red Base:

Apply a smooth, even layer of red face paint over the entire upper portion of the face using a sponge, creating a mask-like shape that covers the forehead, eyes, and upper cheeks. Leave the area around the mouth and chin clean.

2.Black Eye Mask:

With a medium brush, apply black face paint around the eyes, blending it out to create a dramatic, winged effect that extends towards the temples. This black area should be shaped like a bat or flame, giving an intense and fiery appearance.

3.Forehead Design:

Using a thin brush, paint intricate black designs on the forehead that resemble flames or tribal markings. These designs should complement the shape of the black eye mask and add to the devilish theme.

4.Lip and Cheek Details:

Apply red or black lipstick to the lips, keeping the look bold and striking.

Add small black details along the edges of the red mask on the cheeks, such as swirls or flame-like shapes, to enhance the fiery theme.

5.Final Touches:

Add subtle shading with black paint along the edges of the red areas to create depth and a more three-dimensional appearance.

Ensure all lines are sharp and clean, especially around the eyes and forehead, to maintain the polished and intense look.

6.Accessories:

Complete the look with a devil horns headband to emphasize the demonic theme.

Pair the face paint with red or black earrings and a matching costume, such as a red dress or outfit with black accents, to enhance the overall effect.

7.Tips:

Focus on symmetry, particularly with the forehead design and eye mask, to create a balanced and cohesive look.

Use contrasting colors like red and black to make the design stand out and give it a fiery, infernal vibe.

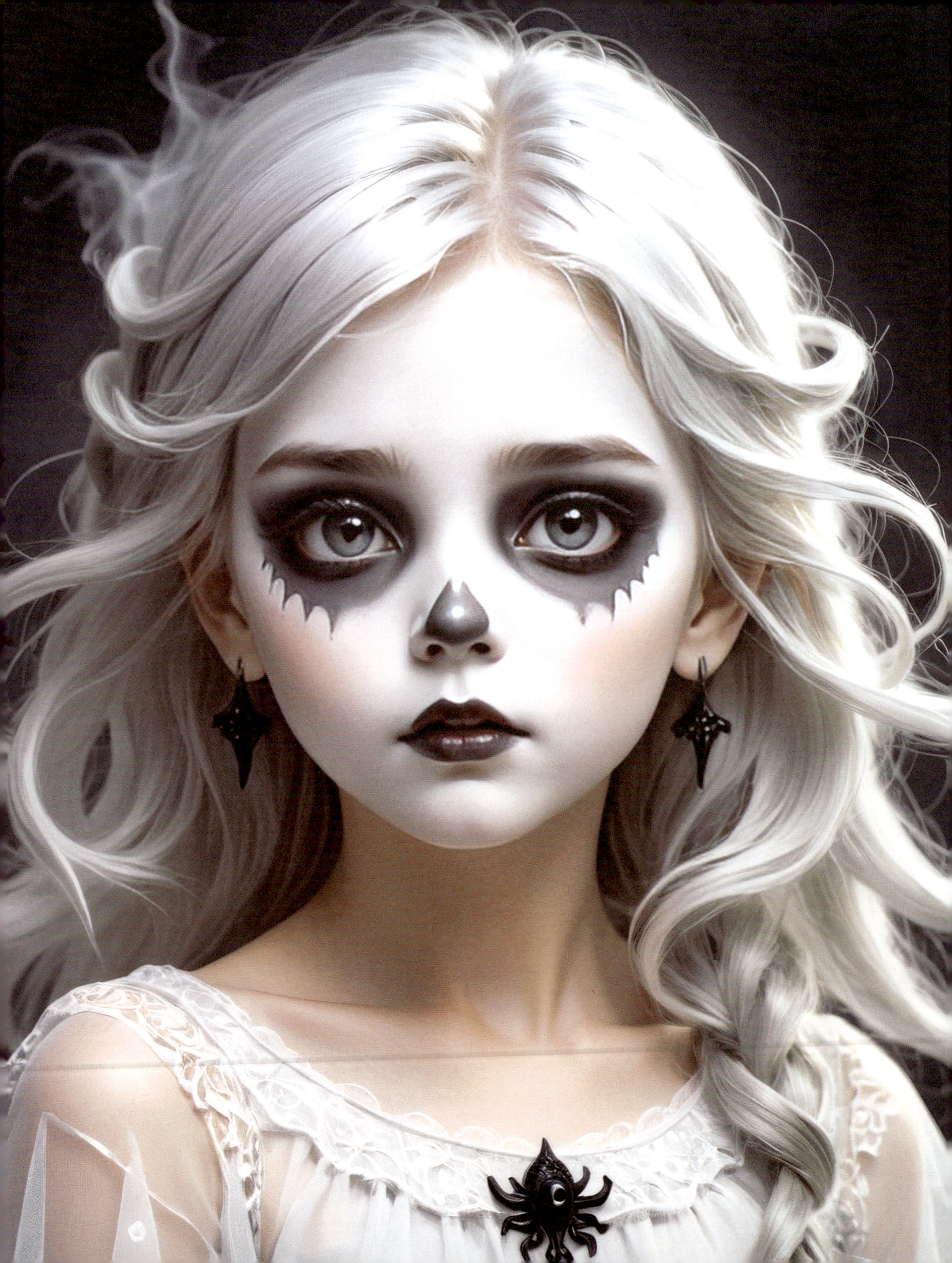

Ghostly Enchantress

Materials:

- Face paints: white, black, grey

- Sponge, thin and medium brushes

- Optional: white wig, gothic black accessories (earrings, brooch)

Steps:

1.White Base:

Apply a smooth, even layer of white face paint over the entire face using a sponge. This creates the ghostly, ethereal foundation that is central to the look.

2.Dark Eye Shading:

Use a medium brush to apply black or dark grey paint around the eyes, blending outward to create a sunken, hollow appearance. Extend the shading slightly beyond the natural eye area, giving the eyes a haunting and intense look.

3.Nose Detail:

Paint the tip of the nose with black face paint in a small, rounded triangle shape, mimicking a skeletal or ghostly appearance.

4.Lip Detail:

Apply black or dark grey lipstick to the lips, keeping the look bold and striking. The lips should have a defined shape, adding to the gothic allure.

5.Subtle Contouring:

Add grey or light black shading along the cheekbones, temples, and jawline to enhance the ghostly, hollowed-out look. Blend carefully to ensure a smooth transition between the white base and the darker areas.

6.Forehead and Cheek Accents:

With a thin brush, add small black or grey details on the forehead and cheeks. These could be small lines, dots, or other minimalist designs that enhance the ghostly theme without overwhelming the face.

7.Final Touches:

Ensure all lines and shading are smooth and well-blended to maintain the ethereal, soft look.

8.Accessories:

Complete the look with a flowing white wig, styled in soft waves or curls to add to the ethereal appearance.

9.Tips:

The key to this look is blending and maintaining a soft, yet striking appearance. Take your time with shading around the eyes and cheekbones to create a hollow, haunting effect.

Keep the black and white elements balanced to ensure the face looks both ghostly and elegant.

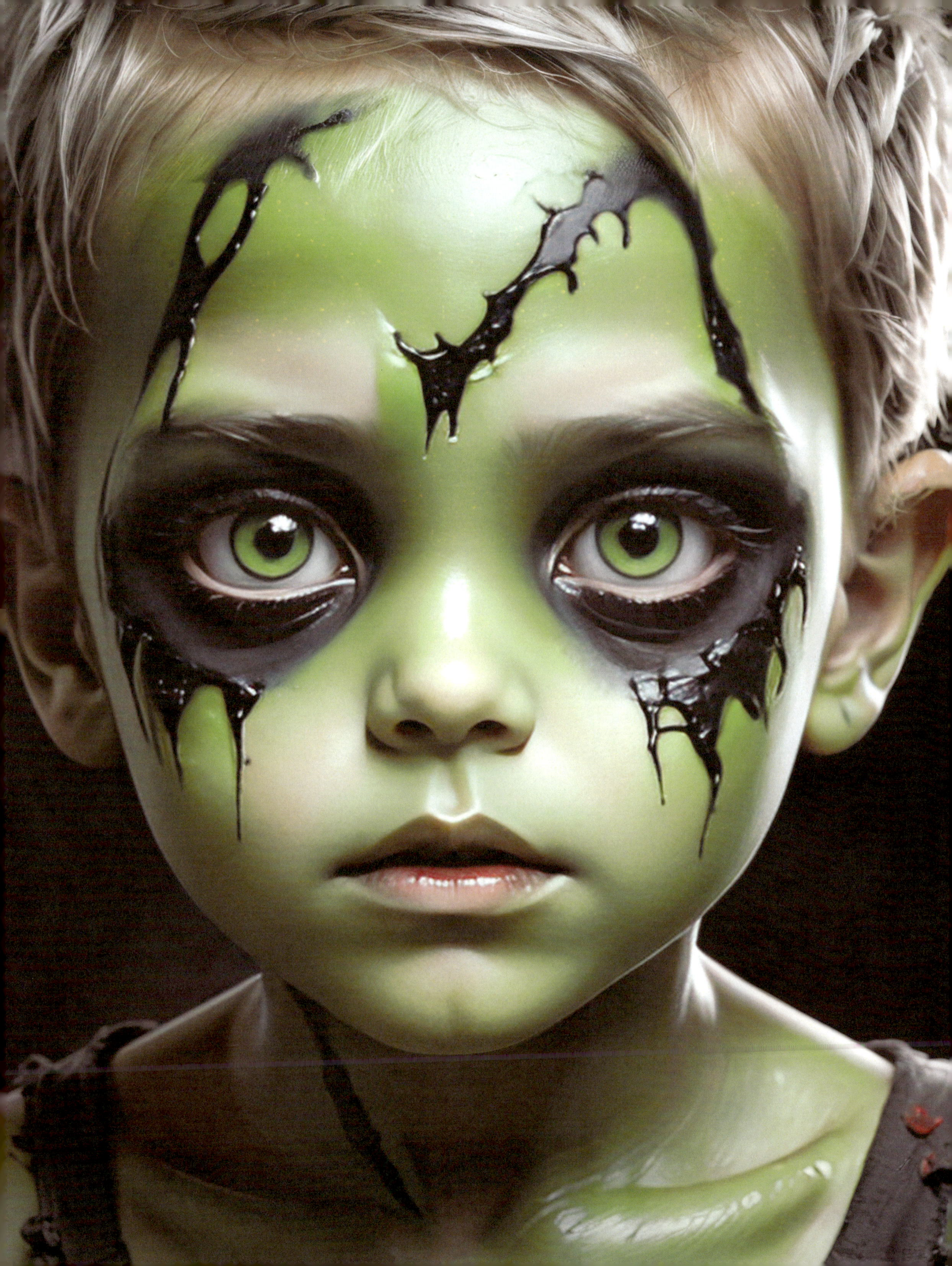

Radioactive Zombie

Materials:

- Face paints: green, black

- Sponge, thin and medium brushes

- Optional: tattered clothing, props to enhance the mutant or zombie look

Steps:

1.Green Base:

Apply a smooth, even layer of green face paint over the entire face using a sponge. This forms the base for the mutated, radioactive appearance.

2.Dark Eye Shading:

Use a medium brush to apply black face paint around the eyes, blending outward to create deep, hollow-looking eye sockets. This will give the eyes a sunken, eerie appearance typical of a zombie or mutant.

3.Dripping Black Marks:

With a thin brush, use black face paint to create dripping, melting marks starting from the forehead and extending down around the eyes and cheeks. These drips should look as though something toxic is oozing down the face.

Make sure the drips vary in length and thickness to add realism and dimension to the design.

4.Forehead and Cheekbone Accents:

Add more detailed black cracks or scars on the forehead and cheeks to enhance the appearance of a deteriorating, mutated face.

5.Final Touches:

Go over the black areas with a bit of dark green or lighter green to add depth and highlight the areas around the drips and cracks.

Blend the black into the green base where necessary to ensure a smooth transition between the colors.

6.Accessories:

Pair the face paint with tattered or distressed clothing to complete the look. The clothes can be slightly torn and stained to match the theme of a mutated or infected character.

Adding fake wounds, dirt, or other accessories can enhance the overall appearance, making the character look more authentic and frightening.

7.Tips:

Focus on creating smooth, realistic drips and blending the colors well to give the impression that the skin is melting or deteriorating.

Use contrasting dark and light green tones to add depth to the face, making the overall look more dynamic and intense.

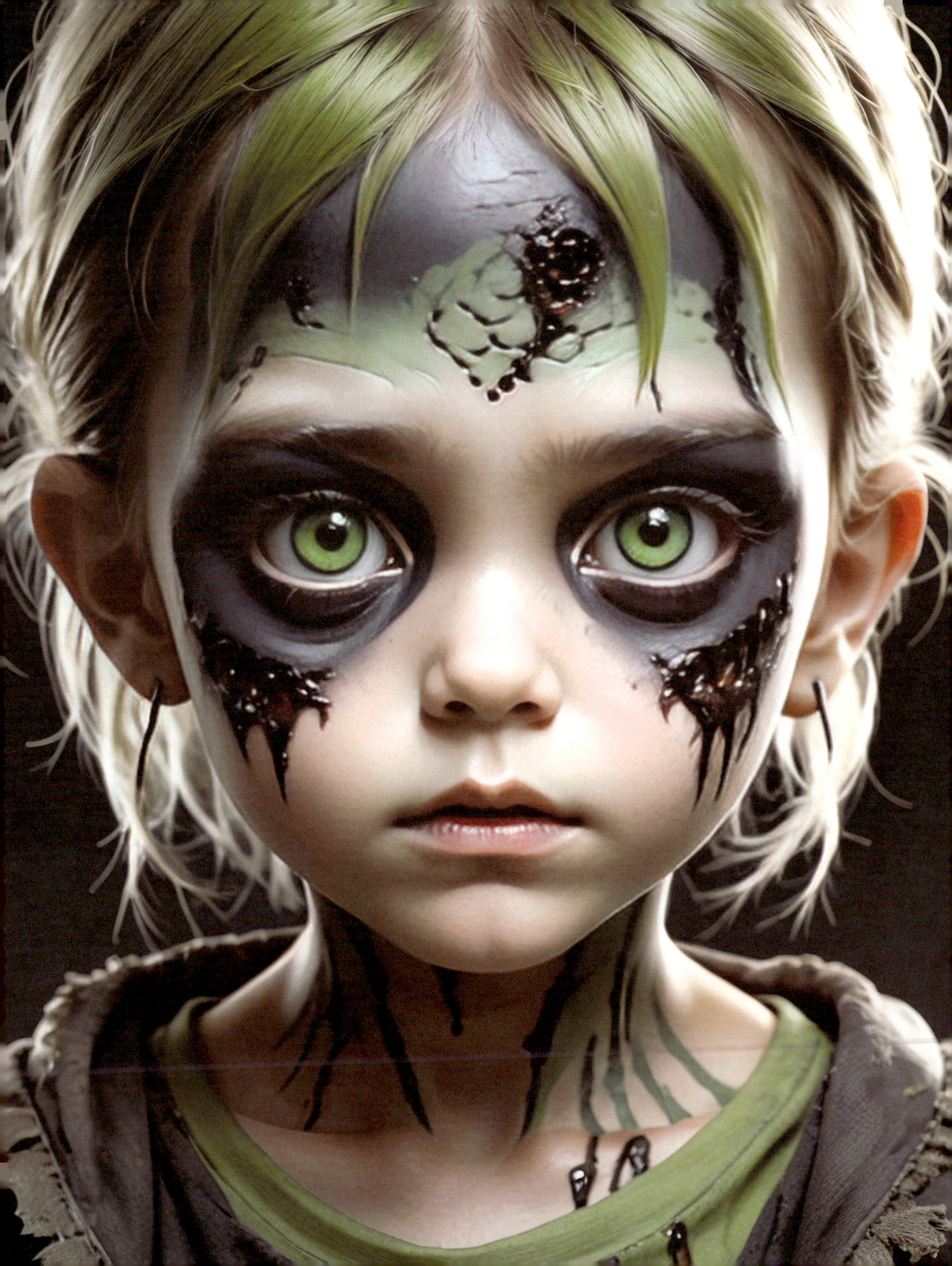

Creeping Plague

Materials:

- Face paints: green, black, dark red

- Sponge, thin and medium brushes

- Optional: distressed clothing, fake wounds, and grime effects

Steps:

1.Green and Black Base:

Start by applying a mix of green and black face paint across the forehead and around the eyes using a sponge. Blend the colors to create a mottled, diseased look. The green should dominate, with black used for shadowing and depth around the eyes and forehead.

2.Eye Shading:

Use a medium brush to apply black face paint heavily around the eyes, extending it outward to create deep, hollow sockets. Blend the black paint to soften the edges, giving a sunken and tired appearance.

3.Forehead Wound:

On the forehead, use black and dark red face paint to create a realistic wound. Start by outlining the wound with black, then fill it in with red. Add small details with a fine brush to make it look infected, such as using a mix of red and black to simulate blood and pus.

4.Cheek and Neck Wounds:

Repeat the wound effect on the cheeks, adding dripping details with black and red paint to give the appearance of infected cuts or sores.

5.Drips and Cracks:

Add additional dripping effects under the eyes and on the neck using black and dark green paint. These should look like something toxic or diseased is leaking from the skin.

Create cracks or creases around the forehead and cheeks with black paint to mimic the appearance of decaying skin.

6.Final Touches:

Use a combination of green, black, and red paint to add subtle shading and highlights around the wounds and eyes. This will give the face a more three-dimensional and realistic appearance.

7.Accessories:

Pair the face paint with distressed clothing that looks worn and dirty, as if the character has been through a lot. Adding grime or fake blood to the clothing can enhance the overall look.

8.Tips:

Focus on blending the black and green tones smoothly to create a realistic, diseased skin effect.

The wounds should look as though they are part of the skin, so take care to blend them well and add appropriate shading.